I0020042

Machine Learning

Study Deep Learning Through Data Science

(Step by Step Guide to Machine Learning Techniques for Beginners)

Michael Krauss

Published By **Regina Loviusher**

Michael Krauss

Machine Learning: Study Deep Learning Through Data Science (Step by Step Guide to Machine Learning Techniques for Beginners)

ISBN   978-1-7773611-6-7

No part of this guidebook shall be reproduced in any form without permission in writing from the publisher except in the case of brief quotations embodied in critical articles or reviews.

Legal & Disclaimer

Table Of Contents

Chapter 1: Classification

Basics of Machine Learning

Jane changed into having lunch with a few pals whilst she have become requested to percent about what she's presently operating on at paintings. She responded, "Machine getting to know." Her friends just checked out her in marvel and that they had been like, "Guys, what's tool reading?" One buddy spoke back, "Cyber dyne Systems T-800." Has everybody of you visible the movie Terminator? It narrates a story of a robot that went towards its programming intelligence. Some of Jane's friend were already remove. This e-book isn't going to try and get into conversations about computer applications or the popularity of synthetic intelligence within the present day international. When we get to tool mastering, an entire new worldwide involves lifestyles because of how the concept of datasets in machines, brings notion into records. This is our definition of learning, no longer the advent of sentient beings nor cyborg rote memorization.

Machine mastering is presently in use, probable in places which you can least assume. Let's have a examine how a everyday day looks as if while you are interacting with machine getting to know without you knowing it. Maybe it's far one in every of your buddy's graduation ceremony and you're planning to shop for a present, and you don't have any clue at the triumphing that you will buy. You visit the internet and look for the extraordinary gift and several applicable links are displayed. When you search for a card in the are searching for engine, there are approximately ten relevant hyperlinks that pop up. When you click on any hyperlink, it will probably be factored in the are seeking out engine to be able to begin a technique of bearing on what you are looking for. Next, whilst you test your emails, the junk mail folder can be stocked with a few loopy adverts approximately offers of merchandise which you is probably inquisitive about.

Next, while you head to the mall to shop for the gift, you buy some towels to your family because you want to update the antique ones. When you get to the cashier to pay for the items, you are offered a discount of $2 for a % of cleaning soap. The coupon have become created through the check in at the cashier's desk, for absolutely everyone who turned into going to shop for a towel. Looking at any other instance, while you make a decision to get a mortgage from a bank, the machine is typically smooth; bankers commonly get right of access for your economic data from their laptop database and determine whether or not or not to provide you a loan, or no longer.

In all of the scenarios we've had been given checked out, there has been the presence of device analyzing. Companies are using tool mastering to enhance and exchange the way business enterprise strategies are finished in all relevant fields of producing. Technology is growing at a velocity most human beings aren't capable of preserve up with. This is making organizations evolve and create new commercial enterprise agency possibilities which might be more facts driven for every the past and destiny facts.

Are you prepared for device gaining knowledge of? You are going to discover what device analyzing is, wherein it's far being used to your everyday every day sports, and the way it is probably of assist to you unexpectedly. Lastly, we're able to speak about not unusual procedures at the manner to solve issues using tool studying.

What is Machine Learning?

You can't make some issue out of numbers if you have masses of information to observe, it'll surely be a blur. Machine studying is ready making feel of data that you were given. It embodies closely on technological know-how and mathematics, no longer to overlook different disciplines that come into play occasionally. There are such a number of possible packages of this manner to trade how we stay on a every day basis. Every area survives on data and the way to apply the statistics to development the development of answers. It is; therefore, secure to mention that tool studying is paramount in each field.

Statistics are the necessities of gadget getting to know. To many humans, statistics is esoteric to companies that need to lie about to clients about how awesome their merchandise are. There is even a ebook at the way to for this the usage of information. So, one might ask, why are records that crucial? The challenge of engineering is the manner to comply with technological understand-the way to problem-fixing. We are used to solving deterministic issues in engineering wherein our answer normally counter our issues all the time.

In this global, we've got issues that we do not even understand in whole intensity. In the 1900's, we had been studying facts with very massive pc structures that have been no longer capable of coping with masses statistics. As time progressed, we've got got come up with superior era, however on the identical time, we've got quadrupled the size of statistics. We cannot system all the information in any given hassle to recognize upcoming or overgrown troubles, with all this information that maintain popping each minute of the day. For example, it's miles difficult to model the inducement of human beings.

In the social sciences place, having 60% accuracy is considered as a a fulfillment degree all of the time. We have not even managed to get to that restrict, now not to say breaking that ceiling.

1. Data deluge and the software program of sensors

Over the very last decade, we have created extra records than the world has ever created given that the begin of time. This is all thanks to the arena massive internet, but of past due, there was a growing quantity of nonhuman statistics resources coming on line. The technology that runs at the back of the sensors has been in lifestyles; however what's new is connecting them to the arena massive internet. Let us observe the following examples to find out approximately information.

A) In 1989, a deadly earthquake struck in the North of California, and it killed loads and injured thousands. Similarly, an earthquake struck Haiti and killed over hundred, 000 human beings in 2010. After the earthquakes occur, scientist analyzed the facts from the earthquakes and that they were able to are looking ahead to the subsequent earthquakes.

B) a few research showed that there was a flaw inside the authentic check on the earthquakes. The issue is, it is very high priced to redo this type of study due to the reality you need to thing in, how the have a have a take a look at might be executed, the device desired, the land for you to be used for the have a check. It's very traumatic making plans for the kind of have a examine. Alternatively, in choice to burdening with the weight, the authorities may be asked to are to be had and assist out. The government may also additionally need to deliver a plot of land and some economic backing wherein the tool will be placed. But though, that is a highly-priced solution that can not get up that regularly, specifically nearly about bringing together one-of-a-type stakeholders.

To counter the luxurious exercising, you could use smartphones to get all the statistics you need. Today, smartphones have built in three-axis magnetometers. The smartphones are filled with executable applications that help in analyzing magnetometers' readings. In addition to the magnetometers, smartphones additionally have dozens of sensors which includes three-axis accelerometers, yaw charge gyros, GPS receivers and temperature sensors, all of that can assist adopt the primary measurements.

The dispositions of sensor-generated statistics and mobile computing way that we are going to have more statistics within the destiny to come back returned.

2. The importance of device studying for the future

Manual tough artwork has out of place its footprint in the ultimate twenty years, way to the upward thrust of the facts age. Job assignments have shifted from the bodily attributes of labor to the conceptual and extra earnings based framework. Business has emerge as even difficult due to the proliferation of facts through the World Wide Web.

This has created an opening of information miners and analyst whose obligations is to assist to analyze statistics for employer use. Currently, companies who're builders of software application have developed software application packages that help business enterprise makes feel of large records from any channel of statistics series. The ability to synthesize information is going to be a mainly type out skill in the close to future. This manner that information this is collected from the critical faculties, excessive schools, faculties and professional institutions ought to be understood and supplied to make knowledgeable alternatives.

The records desire to visualized so as for people to understand it even extra, and put in force it effectively. Managers need to have get right of get admission to to to the information and apprehend it, it's miles even extra important to have people who have the right abilties to talk analyzed records to managers. Data collection turns into more clean to be processed and understood, way to device analyzing. Below are commonplace terminologies which can be decided in system learning that we have to mention in advance than going any similarly.

Key terminology

Before we dive into tool reading algorithms, it is awesome if we recognize terminologies on this vicinity. The extraordinary way to move approximately it's far going via a potential system. Our software is a reptile elegance tool. This is a modern region this is exciting to create a system getting to know algorithm to make clean to categorise reptiles. With the help of computer professionals, laptop software software can be developed to learn how to discover reptiles. Using these sorts of traits, you may determine to degree weight, tail length, whether or not or no longer it has webbed toes, the teeth shape and various factors like poisonous glands. In reality, you will want to degree extra information than what we have were given indexed.

With maximum of those attributes converting, how will the software apprehend which reptile is what? This is in which the term magnificence comes into play. To gain magnificence, computer device gaining knowledge of algorithms. Its common exercising degree pretty a bargain a few element you can degree and kind out the critical elements later.

The four subjects we've measured are known as abilities; the ones also are known as attributes. For the immediate, assume we've got were given were given all of the data from the reptiles. How are we able to flow ahead and decide if a reptile is a frog or something else? This is what is known as magnificence, and currently, there are various gadget reading algorithms that paintings fantastically well at class. We are hereby looking at reptiles and whilst you keep in mind that there are one among a type kind, we're able to recognition on amphibians for this example have a look at.

Once we've the set of rules in region, we need to feed it with training gadgets for it to research on how to distinguish reptiles. A nominal value is a variable that is applied in regression due to the fact its charge is non-forestall. Now, in a training set, its aim price is already said. This is now wherein the system learning algorithms become active. When the record is fed, the algorithms will start constructing relationships a number of the attributes and the aim variable. Now, in our instance, the species is our purpose variable and we're able to slim it down similarly, via way of taking nominal values.

It is essential to be conscious that a schooling set is a easy size that is typically blended with competencies within the set of policies. To test this system getting to know algorithms, there are first-rate gadgets of data which can be desired, the ones are, a schooling set and a check data. The software program is first positioned with a reason variable from the check set of data which enables this device decide the elegance that the best software belongs to. At this thing, the expected rate is in comparison to the goal cost and we then apprehend the right effects of the set of rules.

In our magnificence example, if the consequences pop out as predicted, you may be in a notable feature to say what the gadget has positioned out. This expertise example isn't generally correct. This is because of the truth a few information instance is not understandable thru us. At instances the effects are a tough and rapid of policies or a mathematical equation.

With the set of rules in region, it is time to create a strong software program that is working, from a device language set of regulations. It's time to introduce the topic of regression. Regression basically, is a way to expect a numerical charge. The maximum commonplace clarification of regression even to a primary university is, drawing a remarkable-fit line that explains or attracts a conclusion to data points.

When we talk about Supervised studying, critical additives fall into the elegance, regression, and kind. Supervised learning also can be defined as at the same time as we tell the algorithms what to expect. There is no target fee or label to your statistics class are times of supervised mastering. When we are telling the set of policies what to are looking forward to that is known as supervised gaining knowledge of.

When we communicate about unsupervised studying, we are talking about the absence of a label or target rate for the information. That is in which we need to gather the statistical values for statistics illustration- density estimation. This kind of mastering is tasked to reduce the records to small values that can be decided in dimensions.

How to pick out the Right Algorithm

When writing an set of regulations, you need to have specially defined goals. You might be developing a gadget that predicts the climate tomorrow or a system to pick out the right video games to move for in a betting activity. Any answer you are trying to examine desires a whole lot of information that is precise to it. When you've got defined values like this, you may want to be on supervised learning, otherwise, you can need to remember unsupervised gaining knowledge of. In supervised reading, you may want to have a aim charge. It must be described, like black or white or Yes and No. You might also moreover even want to check out its class at this factor.

If you've got got numerical aim values like permits do not forget -888 to 888, or 1 to 1000, regression is what is advised at this component. Now, whilst you want to restore a few statistics in corporations that you have already established and described, then clustering Is what wishes to be performed. Another manner to categories facts is thru density estimation set of regulations that is when you have numerical records estimates that want to inform mainly groups.

All those guidelines are not constant to, but you recognize the direction we are searching into. It is vital to recognize the statistics in order in your software program to art work as predicted. To help you understand what your statistics need to be like, allows take a glance some questions that you want to invite yourself about the statistics you are jogging on:

Are there any missing values?

Why is there missing facts?

Are there outliers in the records?

Is the records nominal or non-forestall?

Are you searching out non life data?

When you solution those questions, you'll have a greater described set of statistics to help you to construct the set of rules greater without troubles.

It isn't smooth to answer maximum of those questions and offer you with the unmarried tremendous appropriate technique to deciding on the right set of rules, you can have to test specific algorithms and keep in mind the results of every set of guidelines. You can now fantastic trust the strategies which may be applied in machine getting to know. There are even extra tactics to tweak and enhance the overall performance of tool mastering algorithms.

Once the process is finished, you may pick the first rate appearing algorithms, perhaps two will provide superb outcomes and although check more on the ones. You need to understand that the approach of finding the right set of rules goals a repetitive manner this is free of mistakes.

Algorithms have a general number one define of the way all of them are built, even though the stop consequences are awesome. When you give you the algorithms, you may want quite a few these algorithms with a view to benefit a not unusual purpose, what we call a functioning software program.

Let us take a look at the suggestions beneath to approach and construct a device studying software.

1. Collect the information. Use any approach possible to get the right statistics. You need to have a collective tool to check your blood glucose ranges or a few different aspect you need to diploma. The alternatives are limitless. To maintain time, it is possible to use public information that is to be had.

2. Input data guidance. This is to confirm that your facts is of the proper format in advance than the usage of it. One not unusual listing is the Python listing. The benefit of a Python listing is that you probable can blend and healthy facts property and algorithms.

3. Analyze the facts enter. Cross test if the records is in complete and there are not any empty values.

4. In case you are taking walks on a production device, and you've got got a clue about how the facts need to look like, you can skip this step if you agree with its deliver. This step isn't applicable for an automatic tool.

5. Training the set of rules. Machine learning takes place at this diploma. You feed the set of regulations with some clean data from the primary two steps, and then you definately definately extract information from it. This consists of extracting statistics that has already been parsed within the algorithm. The statistics is then saved in a usable layout that the system can access without issues. In

unsupervised mastering, there may be no training step because of the fact no target price exists. The next step uses the whole lot.

6.   Testing the set of guidelines. Test the overall normal performance of the set of policies. In supervised studying, there are diagnosed values that examine an set of guidelines. You can then use every one-of-a-kind set of metrics to assess the set of guidelines, that is unsupervised getting to know. In both case, in case you need one-of-a-kind effects, you may move back to step 4, check once more after converting a few topics. Often the data collection also can had been hard, and you'll need to jump to step 1.

7.   Using it. Here, you are making software that plays a feature.

Probability Theory Classification Using Naive Bayes

In the actual application surroundings, a classifier can make difficult decisions. One can ask for some unique method to the question, for example, we are able to ask, "Which splendor does this case of facts belong to?" There are times while the classifier gets the answer incorrect. In these times, we are able to ask the classifier to offer us a awesome guess about the splendor and a chance estimate assigned to the pleasant wager.

Many device-reading algorithms have the opportunity idea as its basis, so it is crucial to recognise the topic properly. We are going to observe some processes that risk concept may be of service even as classifying matters. We start with the clean probabilistic classifier, make some assumptions and research extra approximately the naïve Bayes classifier. It is given the decision naïve because it formulates naïve assumptions. This can be clean in a while. We will take whole gain of the text-processing capabilities of Python's that lets in to break up a document to a word vector. This is important to classify textual content. We will assemble each extraordinary classifier use it inside the actual global and be aware the way it plays in unsolicited mail email dataset. In case you need a refresher, we are able to evaluation conditional danger

Classification with Bayesian Decision Theory

An Advantage of Naïve Bayes

It performs quite properly with small bits of records

A drawback of Naïve Bayes

There is a want for attention to the detail almost about the statistics inputs. The first-rate values to art work with is the nominal values

What is Bayes?

It is a opportunity interpretation we use that belongs to a category called Bayesian opportunity; it certainly works properly, and it is well-known. Thomas

Bayes, a theologian in the eighteenth-century theologian, have become the founding father of the Bayesian opportunity. In Bayesian chance, it's miles allowed to use not unusual experience and former facts to unsure statements. Frequency possibility is each other interpretation which draws conclusions from information, and it does no longer allow for commonplace experience and earlier know-how.

Conditional Probability

Let's make the effort and speak about conditional hazard and opportunity.

Let us anticipate that we have were given a jar that has 7 balls. Three balls are grey at the same time as four balls are black. If we stick a hand into the jar and pull out one ball at random, what are the possibilities that we pull out a gray ball? There are 7 viable balls, and we have 3 which might be grey. Therefore, the danger is 3/7. What is the opportunity of grabbing a black ball? It's 4/7. We then write the possibility of gray as P(gray). We have calculated the danger of pulling a gray ball P(grey) with the resource of using counting the gray balls and dividing the discern with the useful resource of the entire wide variety of balls.

What if there are seven balls in two jars?

If you want to calculate the P(black) or P(gray), could get to recognize the bucket change the answer? If you desired to compute the opportunity of pulling a grey stone from jar B, you may come what might also additionally figure the way to do this. This is what's known as conditional danger. We are calculating the opportunity of a grey ball, supplied that the unknown ball comes from jar B.

This can be written as:

P(greyjarB), and this it would observe as "the risk of grey given jar B." It is easy to appearance that P(grayjarA) is /four and

P(graythree.

To compute the conditional opportunity, we have got

P(greygrey and jarB)/P(jarB)

Let's take a look at if there can be a few experience in this: P(grey and jarB) = 1/7. This become calculated with the aid of way of the variety of gray balls in jar B and dividing through using the full form of jars. Now,

P(jarB) is three/7 because there are 3 balls in jar B of the entire 7 balls.

Finally, P(grayjarB) = P(grey and jarB)/P(jarB) = (1/7) / (three/7) = 1/3.

This definition looks as if it's an excessive amount of artwork for this example, however it's far going to be beneficial even as more functions are introduced. It is also useful to have this definition if we want to manipulate the conditional opportunity algebraically.

Another important way to manipulate conditional possibilities is called Bayes' rule.

Bayes' rule describes to us the way to change the symbols in a conditional opportunity announcement.

Document beauty with Naïve Bayes

Automatic document class is one important software of tool getting to know, the entire document that's like an individual email is our instance, and its talents are the contents of that e-mail. Email is an example that maintains stoning up, but you could classify message board discussions, information recollections, filings with the government, or any text. You can use terms to check the files and feature a function, the absence or presence of every phrase. This would possibly come up with numerous capabilities. Naïve Bayes is a well-known set of regulations for the report-beauty hassle.

We are going to apply individual terms as skills and look for the absence or presence of each phrase. Which (human) Language are we assuming? How many capabilities is that? It can be more than one language. The preferred big type of terms inside the English language is approximately over 500,000. To take a look at in English, it's miles stated which you want to apprehend loads of phrases. Assuming that our vocabulary is

1,000 words extended. To produce accurate risk distributions, we need some data samples. Let us use N because of the fact the huge form of samples. Statistics display us that if for one characteristic, we want N samples, then for 10 functions we need N10 and for our 1,000-function Vocabulary, we need N1000. The range gets huge right away.

If we expect statistical independence, then our N1000 records points are decreased to a thousand*N. One word or function is simply as probable via way of itself as it is subsequent to exclusive phrases. If we expect that the word bacon goes to appear subsequent to the phrase horrible because of the fact it's miles subsequent to scrumptious, this assumption isn't proper; due to the truth we recognize that bacon nearly usually seems close to delicious but now not close to dangerous. This is what is supposed thru naïve within the naïve Bayes classifier.

One assumption we make is that every characteristic is important which isn't always proper. If we were to categorise a message board posting as beside the point, we simplest want to examine perhaps 10 or 20 and now not to check 1,000 phrases. Despite the assumptions' flaws, naïve Bayes does nicely almost. At this component, you could get into some code with the fundamentals you have got have been given received about this subject matter.

How to technique to naïve Bayes

1. Data series: We can use RSS feeds for instance.

2. Preparation: Boolean or Numeric values.

3. Analyze: Looking at histograms is a higher idea even as looking at many competencies

four. Training: You will want to carry out calculations of the independent attributes to find out the conditional possibilities of impartial skills.

5. Test: Calculate the mistake fee.

6. Implementation: Naïve Bayes may be utilized in any type putting, no longer usually in a text.

four.Five Classifying Text With Python

To get capabilities from our text, the text needs to be split up. But a way to do this is the question. Our talents are going to be tokens from the textual content. A token is any character aggregate. Think of tokens as phrases, but we also can use particular characters which are not phrases collectively with IP addresses, URLs or every exclusive set of characters. We'll lessen every textual content to a vector of tokens wherein the token present inside the report is represented thru 1 and 0 represents its absence.

Let's make a brief easy out to see this in motion. This easy out is on a web message board that flags an irrelevant message if the author makes use of abusive or terrible language. This type of filtering is not unusual because of the fact poor postings can harm an internet network;'s on-line reputation. We are going to have schooling: abusive and no longer abusive. We'll use 1 to represent abusive and zero to symbolize no longer abusive.

First, we're going to create a vector of numbers from redecorate lists of textual content.

Next, from these vectors, we can display the way to compute conditional opportunities.

Then, we will create a classifier and then test practical issues at the manner to implement naïve Bayes in Python.

Preparation: Making Word Vectors from Text

We are clearly going to check the text in terms of token vectors or phrase vectors, and notice how we are able to redesign a sentence to become a vector. All the phrases in our files may be taken into consideration after which we're able to determine what we will use for a hard and rapid of phrases or vocabulary that we are able to recall. Next, we are able to remodel every file to a vector from a vocabulary.

Now we are capable of examine the capabilities being actualised. Save bayes.Py, and enter the following into your Python shell:

import bayes

listOPosts,listClasses = bayes.LoadDataSet()

myVocabList = bayes.Create VocabuList(listOPosts)

myVocabList

['lovable', 'love', 'help', 'garbage', 'give up', 'I', 'problems', 'is', 'park',

'prevent', 'flea', 'hound', 'licks', 'food', 'not', 'him', 'purchasing for',

'posting', 'has', 'nugatory', 'ate', 'to', 'maybe', 'please', 'dog',

'how', 'stupid', 'so', 'take', 'mr', 'steak', 'my']

After studying this list, you may see no repeated phrases. The list is

unsorted, and in case you need to kind it, you may do this later.

Let's have a have a examine the subsequent feature setOfWords2Vec():

bayes.SetOfWords2Vec(myVocabList, listOPosts[0])

[0, 0, 1, 0, 0, 0, 1, zero, 0, 0, 1, zero, 0, zero, zero, 0, zero, zero, 1, zero, zero, zero, zero, 1, 1,

0, zero, 0, zero, zero, zero, 1]

bayes.SetOfWords2Vec(myVocabList, listOPosts[3])

[0, 0, 0, 1, zero, zero, 0, 0, zero, 1, zero, 0, 0, zero, 0, 0, zero, 1, zero, 1, zero, 0, 0, zero, 0,

0, 1, 0, 0, zero, zero, zero]

Create a vector

D of all 0s

This has taken our vocabulary listing which you would really like to take a look at and create a feature for every of them. Now whilst you practice a given record (a posting to

the hound website online), it will probably be converted to a phrase vector. Check to appearance if this makes revel in. What's the phrase at index 2 in myVocabList? It need to help. This word must be in our first record. Now test to see that it isn't in our fourth record.

Logistic Regression

If you consider it, we constantly look at techniques we're capable of optimize troubles in our daily lives. Some optimizations from each day life are those:

How can we adventure from factor A to point B in the shortest time possible?

How are we able to make massive returns or earnings at the same time as doing the least amount of exertions?

How are we able to format a immoderate-common common overall performance engine that produces the most horsepower the usage of the least quantity of fuel?

Optimization has made it viable for us to do powerful subjects. We are going to have a look at severa optimization algorithms to teach a nonlinear function for sophistication.

If regression isn't always familiar to you, it's terrific. You may moreover have visible a few records factors on a graph, and then someone locations the amazing-healthy line to those factors; that's what we call regression. In logistic regression, there may be a bunch of data, and an equation is constructed to perform a type with the records. The regression components endorse that we've got a take a look at locating a nice-in shape set of parameters. Finding the great in form is much like regression, and this is how we train our classifier. We'll use optimization algorithms to discover these extraordinary-match parameters.

How To Approach Logistic Regression

1. Data series: any technique may be used

2. Preparation: for a distance calculation, use Numeric values. It is great to apply a hooked up information format.

three. Analyze: use any technique.

4. Training: maximum of the time can be spent schooling, wherein most suitable coefficients to categorise our data may be checked out.

five. Testing: Classification is rapid and smooth as quickly as the training step is over.

6. Using: This utility wishes a few input data, and an output based totally numeric values.Then, the utility applies simple regression calculation on

the enter information and determines the destined input facts elegance it belongs to. Some movement at the calculated beauty is taken via the software program software.

Preparation: Dealing With Missing Values inside the Data

If you have got were given records and there are missing values, it is a huge hassle, and there are textbooks committed to solving this issue. Well, why is it a hassle? Let's take an instance where we have a hundred instances with 20 features, and a device amassed the facts. What if a tool's sensor have become broken and a characteristic have come to be useless? Is all of the records disposable? What of the 19 specific talents which can be closing; are they any more relevant? Yes, they do. Data is luxurious every now and then, and throwing all of it out isn't always an opportunity, so you a way desires to be diagnosed to address the hassle.

Here are some options:

Use the endorse fee of the feature from the to be had facts.

A unique rate like -1 is used to fill within the unknown.

Ignore the example.

Similar gadgets use the equal imply price.

To assume the fee, use a few extraordinary tool studying set of regulations.

During the preprocessing, you could decide to do subjects from the list. You can first replace all unknown values with a actual quantity because of the fact that we are using NumPy, and in NumPy arrays can't pass over a charge. The tremendous variety zero have become decided on, which fits nicely for logistic regression. The reasoning is: we want a rate with a purpose to not effect the load while updating. The weights are updated relying on

weights = weights + alpha * mistakes * dataMatrix[randIndex]

If any feature's DataMatrix is 0, then the feature's weight will virtually be weights = weights

Also, this will not effect the mistake time period due to sigmoid(zero)=0.Five, is impartial for sophistication prediction. This, therefore, shows that setting o in places in which there are lacking values allows us to keep away from compromising the studying set of rules on the same time as maintaining our imperfect facts. In a few experience, no capabilities take 0 inside the records; it's far handiest a completely unique value. Second, the check data changed into missing a class label. It's hard to replace a lacking beauty label. This answer is critical whilst using logistic regression, however it's miles possibly not to make sense with kNN.

From its authentic shape, the statistics changed into preprocessed and modified in files. Since we have a top notch optimization set of regulations and a clean set of information, we can located some of those quantities together and assemble a classifier to try to see if we are able to are looking beforehand to whether or not or now not colic can be the purpose of loss of life of a horse.

Test: Classifying with Logistic Regression

With logistic regression no longer a first-rate deal wishes to be completed at the same time as classifying an instance. All one wishes to calculate is the sigmoid of the vector being examined extended via manner of the sooner optimized weights. If the sigmoid produces a rate extra than zero.Five, the beauty is 1, and zero if in any other case.

If the rate of the sigmoid is more than 0.Five, it's taken into consideration a 1; otherwise, it's a zero. The colicTest() is often a standalone function that opens the training set, check set and nicely formats the data. First, the loading of the education set is finished, in which the final column consists of the elegance price. At first, the data can contain 3 beauty values representing what came about to the horse: lived, euthanized or died. For this workout, you may then integrate euthanized and died into a class called "did no longer stay." After loading this data, we are capable of use stocGradAscent1() to calculate the weights vector. After the usage of 500 iterations to educate the weights; it improves normal performance over the default 100 fifty iterations. You can change this charge as anticipated. After calculating the weights, you may load the check set and calculate an blunders fee. ColicTest() is in fact a standalone feature. If it's miles run a couple of instances with its random additives, you can have unique outcomes. If the weights converged in stocGradAscent1(), then no random additives might be available.

The ultimate characteristic takes after the use of the common, multiTest(), and running the feature colicTest() 10 instances. After taking walks test script with some enter data, the evaluation may also look like this.

The statistics had a 35% errors charge after 10 iterations. This grow to be not horrible having 30% of the values lacking. To get results coming near a 20% mistakes price, you can modify the alpha length in stochGradAscent1() and additionally the variety of iterations in colicTest().

Summary

Logistic regression way locating the first rate-wholesome parameters to a nonlinear feature that is termed because the sigmoid.

One of the maximum commonplace optimization algorithms is the gradient ascent.

Finding the nice-in shape parameters calls for techniques of optimization.

Stochastic gradient ascent simplifies the Gradient.

Stochastic gradient ascent uses fewer computing sources in assessment to gradient ascent. Stochastic gradient ascent is an internet set of guidelines that doesn't load facts like batch processing, alternatively, it is able to replace what it has discovered out even as new facts is to be had in.

How to cope with missing values within the records is a primary trouble in device getting to know. There is not any wellknown technique to this query. It is predicated upon to your motive with the statistics. There are a few solutions, and every solution has its professionals and cons.

Upgrading Classification Using AdaBoost Meta-Algorithm

If you're taking location to be in a defining role in which you want to decide on the future of a enterprise, it is obvious for one to depend on numerous evaluations that without a doubt one. Why have to we've got it a few different manner nearly approximately system getting to know? The way this is completed in device gaining knowledge of is through the use of meta-algorithms. These incorporate the combination of diverse algorithms. We are going to take a look at AdaBoost to apprehend what we imply thru the use of this.AdaBoost is considered to the incredible-

supervised getting to know algorithm; it's far a MUST have device that need to be in your toolbox.

Classifiers Using Multiple Samples of the Dataset

There are distinctive algorithms for class which whilst you perform a SWOT evaluation, you could see how vital it's far to combine a couple of classifiers. Meta-algorithms or ensemble strategies come into play in this example. Ensemble strategies take the identical set of policies having superb settings, then they use awesome algorithms, or they're assigned one in every of a type dataset factors to as a minimum one-of-a-type classifiers.

Bagging: A Way to Build Classifiers from Random Data

Bagging which is likewise diagnosed as Bootstrap aggregating is a manner that includes an specific statistics sets element makes a very new dataset. The are normally of the same length.

You will need random examples from the precise dataset "with replacement," because of this the same dataset can be used repetitively. "with opportunity" permits repeated values in a dataset and the modern day set will omit the proper values. A studying set of rules is applied to each dataset after building the S datasets. When classifying a modern-day facts piece, you may take a majority vote with the useful resource of manner of making use of the S classifier.

AdaBoost

Pros: easy to code, Low generalization mistakes, no parameters to alter and it truely works with maximum classifiers,

Cons: It is sensitive to outliers. Works properly with every nominal and Numeric values

There are more superior bagging techniques like random forests. Let us flip our hobby to boosting, which goes nearly the equal way due to the fact the bagging approach.

Boosting

Boosting and bagging are specially comparable techniques. When you get into every strategies, you could find out that the identical classifier is used. When you get to boosting, you'll apprehend that the specific classifiers which can be getting used are educated on a sequential basis. Each new classifier is expert inside the equal way that the previous classifiers were knowledgeable on. When boosting is completed, classifiers are led to concentrate on misclassified information that changed into finished via previous classifiers.

The difference amongst boosting and bagging is available in on output calculations. In boosting, the output calculation comes from the weighted sum of the classifiers which might be in it. When you have a study the weights on bagging and boosting, you may see the difference. In bagging, you have to understand that the out is relying on the achievement of a classifier modified into within the preceding sections. There are very many boosting version, however we are able to attention on AdaBoost, this is the maximum famous model.

How to technique AdaBoost

1. Collection: Find the extremely good manner to acquire the records.

2. Preparation: Choose a vulnerable learner, use desire stumps and use a smooth classifier in this manner.

3. Analyze: There are unique tactics you can test the exceptional of the information.

four. Training: teach the prone novices over and over at the identical dataset.

five. Testing: Test the dataset over and over and take a look at the mistake charges.

6. Use: AdaBoost predicts simply considered one of classes much like guide vector machines.

If you want to apply it for type related to more than education, you may need to practice some of the equal techniques as for assist vector machines.

AdaBoost and help vector machines are the most effective algorithms in supervised mastering. The are similar in multiple techniques. First, the kernel of the help vector machines is the willing learner in AdaBoost. The AdaBoost set of guidelines may be written concerning maximizing a minimal margin. Margins are calculated in unique methods which result in exceptional outcomes majorly close to better dimensions.

Classification Imbalance

Imagine a person brings a horse, asks us to make a prediction on whether or no longer the pony will die or not. If demise is our selection and we're delaying the plain final consequences, then the very last choice is to have the pony euthanized. After all, if we are watching for incorrect, the horse could possibly have lived. If we expected incorrectly our in which our classifier is handiest 80% accurate, we would have subjected the horse to a death penalty.

Let's dive into junk mail detection. It is not even conceivable to allow direct mail emails to get to the inbox. There are many examples of this nature, and we are able to say that the fee is in no way identical.

Sampling of Data and Working Around Classification Imbalance

Classifiers are tuned to trade the statistics that trains classifiers that address imbalanced obligations if classification. This is executed through records undersampling and oversampling.

When we talk approximately undersampling, it method to pattern deleting whilst oversample method to copy samples. Whichever way you pick out, you may be converting information. Sampling is done each randomly or thru a specific structured procedure. Normally, there is an outstanding case of credit score score card fraud which you're in search of to become aware of. You want to preserve sufficient facts about the uncommon case, so you need to store all immoderate extraordinary and undersample examples, and the discard poor examples from the terrible magnificence.

One drawback is deciding on one horrible downside to remove. When you are making the choice on which instance to cast off, you could toss out valuable statistics that isn't always contained the alternative examples.

A solution for that is selecting samples to toss that isn't near the choice boundary. We can take an instance and say which you have a dataset with 50 credit card transactions which might be fraudulent and also you also have transactions which can be valid counting to 5,000. To further stability the set of facts then about 4950 of the legitimate transactions will have to be ignored and removed. Although those examples can also embody critical information and this appears excessive, consequently, it is prudent that a bypass blend approach is used surely so out of the 2 units of samples, oversampling the high excellent set and undersampling of the lousy set is considered as the opportunity opportunity that can be used.

For the oversample of the top notch set, established new elements which are equal to those factors already gift or replicate the triumphing examples. One approach to do not forget is to add one facts factor interpolated in a number of the already present information element. This effects to overfitting.

Summary

Instead of truly using one classifier, ensemble techniques some distance higher tactics for the reason that they integrate the possible consequences of the a couple of classifiers so as to arrive at a more suitable and turning into answer. We have decided to deal with on the techniques the use of remarkable one form of classifier despite the truth that there are combos of techniques that use various styles of classifiers. In blending a couple of classifiers this seeks to make the maximum of the shortcomings of unmarried classifiers, like overfitting. Since the classifiers are special from each unique, combining more than one classifiers can help. This difference can be inside the use of statistics to that set of rules or used to make up the set of regulations. The types of techniques ensembles we discussing are are boosting and bagging. Boosting involves borrowing and taking the concept of bagging greater in addition with the resource of the application of a extraordinary classifier consecutively to a dataset.

When it includes bagging, datasets which can be of comparable length due to the fact the right dataset are made up through sampling examples in a random manner for the dataset with replacement. Random forests are a further ensemble approach efficaciously used. Random forests are not as famous as AdaBoost. AdaBoost makes use of the lowest classifier as a inclined learner, with the weight vector weighing the input facts.

Data is further weighted in the first new release. If information come to be incorrectly labeled formerly, then in the consecutive iterations the information is weighted extra strongly. This is the energy that's related to AdaBoost, its adaptive nature of the mistakes formerly completed. By using AdaBoost, then the capabilities which can be built to create the classifier and preference stumps which are the inclined learner. When the weighted statistics is well appropriated through the classifier, then the capabilities of the AdaBoost may be done to any classifier. The AdaBoost set of guidelines indicates how powerful it's miles by using manner of quick dealing with datasets that specific classifiers decided to be tough. The imbalance hassle of class is schooling a classifier with statistics which the terrible and remarkable examples are not same. The bad and first-rate examples have unique misclassification charges, a problem usually arises.

Chapter 2: Using Regression To Forecast Numeric Values

Tree-based Regression

One way to model our facts is to subdivide it into sections that we're able to use to construct a model without a hassle. Using linear regression strategies, those walls can then be modeled. If we first partition the data and the consequences don't wholesome a linear model, then we will partition the partitions. Recursion and Trees are beneficial gadget nearly approximately partitioning. We will first test CART, a modern day set of policies for constructing wood. CART stands for Classification And Regression Trees. It may be applied to category or regression, so it is a treasured device to examine.

Using CART for Regression

To model complicated statistics interactions, we've were given had been given determined to use trees to partition the records. How will partitions be cut up up? How can we understand while we've got cut up up the facts enough? It all is based upon on how we're modeling the very last values. The regression tree approach makes use of a tree to break up statistics with constant values at the leaf nodes. This method assumes that we will summarize the complicated interactions of the information.

To gather a tree of piecewise steady values, we want to degree the consistency of data. How can we gauge the illness of non-prevent values? It is pretty smooth to degree a disorder for a hard and fast of records. We will should calculate first the imply charge of a hard and speedy and locate the statistics deviation of every piece of this suggest fee. To deal with each pleasant and bad deviations similarly, we want to get the significance of the deviation from the advocate. The significance may be gotten with the squared rate or simply the fee. Calculating the variance could be very commonplace in statistics. The best difference is that the variance is the suggest squared mistakes and we are searching out the overall mistakes. We can get this ordinary squared blunders with the aid of multiplying the variance of a dataset by using using way of the wide range of things in a dataset.

With a tree-building set of guidelines and this error rule, it is viable to put in writing code to gather a regression tree from a dataset.

Tree Pruning

An instance of a version overfit is a tree with too many nodes. Pruning is the way of decreasing the complexity of a desire tree to keep away from overfitting.

Post Pruning

In this method, to start with, you can need to split the statistics right right into a schooling set and a take a look at set. First, you can collect a tree with the putting for you to offer you with the largest, maximum complex tree. You will then descend the tree until you gain a node that has only leaves. You will use a take a look at set to check the leaves in opposition to information and degree if merging the leaves are going to offer you lots an awful lot much less mistakes at the test set. If merging the nodes will reduce the error on the take a look at set, you could merge the nodes.

Pseudo-code for prune() representation:

In a given tree, cut up the test statistics:

If the either cut up is a tree: name prune on that cut up

Compute the error after merging leaf nodes

Without merging, compute the mistake

Merge the leaf nodes if merging consequences is in decrease mistakes

One way to model our records is to subdivide it into sections that we're capable of use to construct a model efficaciously. Using linear regression techniques, these walls can then be modeled. If we first partition the records and the results don't suit a linear model, then we are capable of partition the walls. Recursion and Trees are beneficial gear with reference to partitioning. We will first test

CART, a ultra-cutting-edge set of policies for constructing trees. CART stands for Classification And Regression Trees. It can be accomplished to category or regression, so it's miles a treasured device to look at.

Often, your statistics has complex interactions that lead to nonlinear relationships a few of the enter facts and the goal variables. To version the ones complex relationships, you may use a tree to break up the expected rate into piecewise linear segments or piecewise ordinary segments.

A regression tree is a tree form that fashions the statistics with piecewise everyday segments. If the models are linear regression equations, the tree is known as a version tree.

The CART set of regulations builds binary timber handles non-prevent split values similarly to discrete values. Model wooden and regression trees can be built with the CART algorithm as long as the proper mistakes measurements are used. There is a dishonest for the tree-constructing set of guidelines to construct the tree too near the records at the same time as constructing a tree; this outcomes in an overfit model. There is mostly a form of complexity on the subject of an overfit tree. A approach of pruning is performed to the tree to make it lots a great deal much less complex. Two strategies of pruning are normally available, pre-pruning, which prunes the tree as within the constructing segment, and put up-pruning, which prunes the tree after the building segment is complete. Pre-pruning is greater effective, however it calls for man or woman-defined parameters.

Tkinter is the most usually used GUI toolkit for Python. Tkinter permits one to build widgets and set up them. You can create a special widget for Tkinter that permits you to display Matplotlib plots. The integration of Matplotlib and Tkinter allows you to construct powerful GUIs wherein human beings can discover device gaining knowledge of algorithms greater manifestly.

Chapter 3: Unsupervised Learning

Grouping Items that Are Not Labeled Using K-method Clustering

When strolling a presidential election, it's far possible to have the winner come out victories with a completely small margin from the number one runner up. An example is while the well-known vote that a candidate gets is 50.7%, and the bottom is 47.Nine%. If a specific percent of the residents are to visit the alternative component, then the very last outcomes of the election may be one among a kind. In an election duration, there's business enterprise of electorate who can be pressured to update aspects. These companies can be small, however with near races just like the only we are describing, the businesses may also grow to be big sufficient to adjust the election's final consequences

Now, how does one locate the ones "small" corporations of humans, and the way does one appeal to them with a small rate variety? The choice to this query is clustering. Let us have a study how it's miles executed. First, you may need to accumulate human beings's records with or without their approval: any facts that would offer a clue on what triggers will have an impact on them. Then input the results right right into a clustering set of regulations. Afterward, pick out out the maximum vital first for each cluster and prepare a message at the manner to attraction to them. Finally, you may begin your marketing campaign and track its normal overall performance.

Clustering is mechanically forming corporations of things which is probably similar; it's far a form of unsupervised analyzing, and it's also like an automatic category. You can cluster a few factor, clusters are continuously higher if there are extra similar devices in a single cluster; the extra similar the devices are inside the cluster, the better your clusters are. We are going to have a study one type of clustering set of rules referred to as ok-way. It's called K approach as it reveals good enough particular clusters, and the center of each cluster is the propose of the values in that cluster. You'll see this in greater element in a bit bit.

Before we get into ok-manner, let's talk about cluster identification. Cluster identity tells an set of regulations, "Here's a few facts. Now organization similar topics collectively and tell me about those groups." The key difference from category is that during type you recognize what you're seeking out. That's no longer the case in clustering. Clustering is every so often called unsupervised class as it produces the same end result as class however even as no longer having predefined instructions.

With cluster evaluation, we're attempting to find to placed comparable topics in a cluster and diverse topics in a exquisite cluster. This notion of similarity is based upon on a similarity length. You've seen brilliant similarity measures in previous chapters, and they'll arise in later chapters as well. The kind of similarity degree used is based upon on the software program program. We'll collect the ok-approach set of regulations and see it in motion. We'll next speak a few smooth okay-way set of regulations drawbacks. To art work on a number of those issues, we will comply with post processing to provide higher clusters. Next, you'll see a greater inexperienced model of ok-manner referred to as bisecting adequate-manner. Finally, you'll see an example in which we'll use bisecting good enough-way to find out maximum useful parking locations even as touring more than one nightlife hotspots.

The adequate-manner clustering set of rules

Advantage:

Implementation is easy

Disadvantage:

It is sluggish on massive datasets

The algorithm carries numeric values

It can converge at nearby minima

In the k-approach set of pointers, ok clusters can be located first for a particular dataset. The okay clusters at the way to be determined may be purchaser defined. A single point this is called the centroid describes every cluster. The term Centroid technique that it's positioned the center of all of the elements within the cluster. This is how the adequate-method algorithm works. First, the ok centroids are randomly assigned to a point. Next, every trouble in the dataset is assigned to a cluster. The task is carried out through locating the nearest centroid and assigning the element to that cluster. After this step, the centroids are all updated thru taking the endorse charge of all of the elements in that cluster.

Here's how the pseudo-code should appearance:

Create good enough elements randomly for starting centroids

While any point has modified the cluster cluster

for each dataset aspect:

for each centroid

compute the distance among the thing and the centroid

the cluster is assigned to the aspect with the lowest distance

for every cluster compute the advise of the points in that cluster

the imply is assigned the centroid

General approach to ok-way clustering

1. Collecting: use of numerous facts collection techniques is okay

2. Preparing: Nominal values and distance computing require nominal values

3. Analyze: Use any statistics analysis approach.

four. Training: it's miles great available in supervised mastering five. Testing: Check the output of the clustering set of suggestions all through checking out. You can use Quantitative blunders

Measurements similar to the of squared mistakes.

6. Use: Anything available works.

Bisecting ok-way

An set of rules this is known as bisecting - technique has been developed to counter the horrible clusters trouble. It starts offevolved out with one cluster after which splits the cluster in . It then chooses a cluster to break up. The cluster to interrupt up is determined with the beneficial resource of minimizing the SSE. This splitting based on the SSE is repeated till the consumer-described amount of clusters is received.

Pseudocode for bisecting adequate-manner will seem like this:

Begin with all the elements in a cluster

While cluster numbers is a whole lot much less than k

for each cluster

degree the entire mistakes

ok-manner is then finished with adequate=2 on the given cluster

The general blunders is measured after k-way has break up the cluster in

pick out the cluster cut up that gives the lowest errors and devote this split

Another manner of thinking about this is to choose out the cluster with the most critical SSE and break up it and then repeat until you get to the customer-described big kind of clusters. This doesn't sound too difficult to code, does it? To see this in motion, open kMeans.Py and enter the code from the following listing.

Example: clustering elements on a map

Here's the state of affairs: your friend Drew needs you to take him out in town for his birthday. Some special buddies are going to go back again also, so you want to provide a plan that everyone can observe. Drew has given you a list of locations he desires to skip. This list is lengthy; it has 70 establishments in it. I protected the listing in a record known as portland-Clubs.Txt, that is packaged with the code. The listing carries comparable institutions inside the extra Portland, Oregon, region.

Seventy locations in a single night time! You decide the excellent approach is to cluster the ones locations collectively. You can arrange transportation to the cluster centers after which hit the locations strolling. Drew's listing consists of addresses, but addresses don't offer you with a whole lot of statistics approximately how near two places are. What you need are the range and longitude. Then, you could cluster those places collectively and plan your revel in.

Example: using bisecting ok-method on geographic facts

1. Collect: Use the Yahoo! PlaceFinder API to accumulate facts.

2. Preparation: Remove all statistics except latitude and longitude.

3.Analyze: Use Matplotlib to make 2D plots of our facts, with clusters and map.

four.Train: It is best available in supervised studying.

5. Test: Use biKmeans().

6.Use: The final product may be your map with the clusters and cluster centers.

You need a company for you to convert an cope with to range and longitude. Luckily, Yahoo! Provides the sort of provider. Where you will discover the way to use the Yahoo! PlaceFinder API.

Chapter 4: Where To Go From Here

Career Opportunities

These are a number of the talents one desires to need to take advantage of the ever developing profession opportunities in Machine studying.

1. Fundamentals of Computer Science and Programming

Machine learning is depending on basics which might be studied in pc era. Some of these basics encompass: (sorting, looking, dynamic programming, optimization e.T.C), records structures (queues, timber, multi-dimensional arrays, stacks, graphs e.T.C), computability and complexity (approximate algorithms, huge-O notation, NP-complete issues, P vs. NP and lots of others.), and laptop shape (distributed processing, bandwidth, deadlocks, cache, memory e.T.C)

You should be organized to put in force, address and adapt to the ones fundamentals. When you are programming. To decorate and hone your talents, you want to have interaction in hackathons, coding competitions, and workout issues.

2. Probability and Statistics

Probability dispositions (Bayes rule, independence, conditional opportunity, opportunity, e.T.C) and strategies which can be derived from (Hidden Markov, Markov Decision Processes, Bayes Nets, e.T.C.) the basis of Machine Learning algorithms.

These are the strategies that help in managing real global troubles which might be elusive to us.

To collect a courting with this situation, the maximum relatable location is the sphere of records which has in its provision vital measures much like the median, imply and famous deviation. Distributions that encompass binomial, Poisson, regular and uniform are usable. To upload, assessment techniques like hypothesis testing and ANOVA also are to be had technique important for model building and validation from facts that is decided. For this basis, it's far glaring that system analyzing is an extension of methods which may be in statistical modeling.

three. Evaluation and Data Modeling

When you describe records modeling, what ought to come to thoughts is that it is an estimation technique that happens at the datasets underlying shape, centered on discovering patterns which might be useful. They embody eigenvectors, clusters, correlation e.T.C. Awaiting and speculating homes of unseen instances like regression, anomaly detection, kind e.T.C. An critical a part of this system is the non-prevent assessment of methods a model is. You will should pick out an accuracy measure counting on the challenge you're running on, as an example, sum-of-squared-mistakes for regression, log-loss for class, e.T.C) and a technique evaluation like sequential vs randomized cross-validation or training-finding out break up, e.T.C. Learning algorithms which are iterative right now use emanating mistakes to changing the version like backpropagation on neural networks. Therefore, understanding the measures is critical for even making use of contemporary algorithms.

4. Machine Learning Algorithms and Libraries Application

Machine Learning algorithms popular packages are available thru APIs (e.G. Tensor Flow, Theano, scikit-have a take a look at, Spark MLlib, H2O etc.), applications, libraries. Using them consists of deciding on a appropriate shape, a manner of gaining knowledge of to healthy the records (gradient descent, linear regression, bagging, boosting, algorithms to do with genetics and other version-particular strategies and getting a grip of the way studying is laid low with parameters. You should additionally be acquitted the dangers and benefits of various strategies and gotchas that could adventure one (overfitting and underfitting, bias and variance, facts leakage, lacking facts and plenty of others) Machine Learning challenge and Data Science are interesting techniques to discover new problems and their respective nuances.

5. System Design and Software Engineering

For any Machine Learning Engineer, the normal output is a

software software program. This is part of a larger incorporated device of services and products. One wishes to get how awesome quantities relate (using REST APIs, library calls, database queries, e.T.C) and paintings collectively and assemble interfaces for the ones additives that allows you to make others depend on. It is critical to design cautious tool designs to skip problems and with the growing large information then your algorithms scale with it.

Chapter 5: The Future Of Employment

How Jobs are Susceptible to Computerization

We are going to take a look at the ability destiny dangers that challenge computerization will deliver to the desk and the associated exertions marketplace outcomes. It has been predicted that new tendencies in ML will help to carry down the gathered call for for tough paintings enter in duties that may be routinized via reputation of patterns at the identical time as developing the difficult paintings call for for the ones responsibilities that are not liable to computerization.

It's no longer feasible to expect the destiny modifications in the hard work marketplace, and we don't intend to do this. This is due to the fact, constant with a BLS occupational employment projections that have been executed in 2010, it is difficult to count on US internet employment growth in super business corporation fields primarily based at the historical styles. Technology is starting to proliferate into extremely good sectors, and we can't speculate how a long way generation will effect the economic organisation environment. This method that the information we've on the technological effect remains growing and we want to continuously examine it.

We are at this 2d restricted to how destiny computerization may be state of affairs to substitution. In the subsequent few a long term, tendencies in computerization will generally have a tendency to depend on the progress of the problems described above can be overcome. Looking at it in this form of mindset, the outcomes are comparable in sets of computations which is probably cut up through way of a "technological plateau."

Workers in logistics and transportation occupations, together with the govt. Assist and bulk of administrative center, will symbolize thru the first wave together; and laptop capital can be at the manner of changing manufacturing occupations. We are seeing a upward push in computerized automobiles which has brought about the lower of the immoderate charge of sensors, that makes developing vehicles which have been upgraded with superior sensors, an increasing number of within your budget. The automation of logistics occupations and transportation is going to increase unexpectedly with the tech enhancements coming on board to make it much less complex to deliver devices the world over. We inside the in the meantime are seeing how huge facts algorithms are entering into the domains that store records, making it viable for workplace operations to be undertaking to computerization.

As there may be an increase in business corporation robots which might be advancing in capability and overall performance, they will be tasked with walking non-guide duties during the board. In the subsequent couple of a few years, we also are going to peer a reduce down on production occupations, as this challenge goes to be a far an awful lot much less common employment field. If you examine the landscape with regards to issuer, manufacturing, or even profits occupations, we can also assume to look computerization of those obligations.

Limitations

Our future projections are primarily based on forecasting at the reality that we are going to see computerizations inside the new destiny materializing. Therefore, we are focusing on making an estimate of the employment project that may be modified thru synthetic intelligence.

We will now not make any try and diploma the roles so as to be replaced by using way of laptop structures. There are numerous elements as a manner to cause the real tempo and amount of computerization.

First, if human capital prices are pretty excessive or the get entry to to reasonably-priced tough paintings is scarce, upgrades of creating hard work reasonably-priced can be taken into consideration. For instance, it is been documented that production of cotton in Britain in the eighteenth century, relative to special international locations, Britain's earnings stages were very better. Also, modern empirical studies does not account for capital expenses, tough work shortages or future salary ranges. As those factors have the capability to impact the timeline of our predictions, the scarce thing is tough work. This way that employment is probably growing at once proportional to capital prices, and this may make all computerized operations profitable.

Second, political activism and regulatory worries may additionally moreover slow down the computerization manner. The states of Nevada and California have made a legislative trade to allow for driverless vehicles. Other states are also following in form. The pace and quantity of law are dependent additionally on the development of era that the public is accepting. Although due to the fact the Industrial Revolution, there has been a slowing resistance to technological exchange. We are keeping off to say that technological development, predictive legislative manner and the pace of computerization is apparent to all.

Third, it's far difficult to make predictions approximately technological improvement. This leads us to recognition at the enhancements that we are making in generation, in Machine Learning, to avoid making projections that have a undertaking to overcome numerous engineering bottlenecks in computerization. Finally, we are not going to investigate the mild changes that computerization makes in some small obligations that facilitate the boom of human exertions.

For examples, the previous Britain baby-kisser William Huskisson turned into killed at some point of the hole ceremony of a railway locomotive that changed into being launched in Liverpool and Manchester Railway. This incident dissuaded the overall public from generation in railway transportation. By assessment, generation in an airship is extensively recognized and it misplaced the eye of many veterans within the commercial enterprise company due to the very last results of the Hindenburg catastrophe.

Uber, one of the fasted mobile app organization that has ever existed, connects drivers to passengers, has been criticized through regulators from exceptional global locations due to the price wars that the taxi provider has been experiencing. Marvin Minsky in 1970, famously claimed that "within the subsequent decade we are capable of have a machine with the overall intelligence of a median person." This estimation is but to materialize.

Chapter 6: Machine Learning

Machine learning now fundamentally differs from machine learning in the past, thanks to advancements in computing technology. Researchers in artificial intelligence sought to find if computers could teach from data and were inspired by pattern classification and the hypothesis that computers can study without being trained to execute certain tasks; this was the genesis of artificial intelligence.

The iterative feature of deep learning is significant because as algorithms are exposed to new data, they can adjust independently without human intervention. They learn from their prior computations and use this knowledge to make judgments and create trustworthy and predictable outcomes. A

the science that has been around for a while — and one that has recently acquired momentum. It is the study of algorithms that may improve automatically via experience and data usage, referred to as machine learning (ML). It is a component of artificial intelligence. Machine learning algorithms create a model sample statistic, called training data, in making predictions or choices without being explicitly taught. Computer vision, medicine, email filtering, and speech recognition are just a few fields where machine learning is utilized to solve problems where it is difficult or impossible to create traditional algorithms to accomplish the required tasks. Statistical learning is a type of machine learning related to computer science, which is concerned with making predictions with computers; nevertheless, statistical learning is not all machine learning. The authority of machine learning advantages from the study of optimization techniques since it provides tools, theory, and application domains. Data mining is an intricately connected topic of research that focuses on efficient data mining utilizing unsupervised learning techniques to solve problems. Some machine learning implementations utilize data and artificial neural in a manner intended to simulate the functioning of a physical brain. Machine learning is mentioned as projecting analytics when used to solve business challenges across various industries. The ability to successfully implement artificial intelligence (AI) in the not-so-distant future shown by robots is critical to our ability to create this world. However, changing robots into thinking gadgets is not as straightforward as it may appear.

Strong artificial intelligence (AI) can only be reached through machine learning (ML), which allows robots to comprehend as humans do. Machine learning works similarly to whether the human mind acquires information and understanding; it uses input, such as the testing phase or domain knowledge, to grasp things, domains, and relationships. Deep learning can commence once the entities have been defined. The machine learner can begin with observable data such as samples, direct experience, or instruction. It looks to identify patterns in data to draw conclusions later based on the user's information. The basic goal of machine learning is to enable computers to learn independently, without the need for human interaction or support, and to change their behaviour accordingly. Machine learning works similarly to how the human mind acquires information and understanding: it uses input, such as testing phase or visualization techniques, to grasp things, domains, and their relationships. Deep learning can commence once the entities have been defined. Active machine learning can begin with observable data such as samples, direct experience, or instruction. It searches for patterns in data to draw conclusions later based on the user's examples. The basic goal of machine learning is to enable computers to learn independently, without the need for human interaction or support, and to change their behaviour accordingly.

Arthur Samuel, an American IBMer and prominent pioneer in computer games and artificial intelligence, created the word "machine learning" in 1959. During this period, self-teaching computers were also used as a synonym. Nilsson's work on Learning Machines dealt primarily with machine learning with pattern categorization throughout the

The 1960s is considered a prototypical machine learning book. The interest in pattern recognition persisted well into the 1970s, according to Duda and Hart's 1973 account. When a neural net learns to recognize 40 characters (26 letters, ten digits, and four special characters) from a computer terminal, a report was given in 1981. The study discussed employing teaching methodologies to train the network to recognize the characters.

A more precise definition of algorithms explored in the field of machine learning was provided by Tom M. Mitchell. It is widely quoted: "A computer program is said to understand from knowledge E concerning a certain class of tasks T and achievement was Therefore if its performance exceeds expectations, as evaluated by P, improves as a function of experience E." Instead of describing the area in terms of cognitive concepts, this characterization of the activities in which computer vision is concerned provides a genuinely operational definition of the field. In his work "Computing Machinery and Intelligence," Alan Turing proposes that the question of "Can machines think?" be replaced with the question of "Can machines perform what we (as thinking creatures) can do?" Modern-day machine learning includes two goals: one is to categorize data climate models that have been established, and the other is to predict future trends and events based on the models that have been developed. Machine learning is used to classify data and make predictions about future outcomes. To train an algorithm unique to classifying data, a hypothetical system that combines machine learning of moles with supervised learning may be used to classify malignant moles. In the case of stock trading, a machine learning model may be used to alert the dealer of probable future projections.

Machine Learning is receiving all the attention it deserves right now. Machine Learning has the potential to automate a wide range of operations, particularly those that are only capable of being performed by humans using their intrinsic intellect. This intelligence can only be replicated in machines with the advancement of machine learning, which is now being researched. Businesses can automate ordinary processes with the use of Machine Learning. It also aids in automating data analysis and creating models in a brief period. Data is critical in many businesses since it optimizes operations or makes more informed decisions. Machine Learning aids in developing models capable of processing and analyzing enormous amounts of data to produce accurate results. These models are exact and scalable and can be operated quickly. Developing such accurate machine learning models allows firms to capitalize on economic possibilities while avoiding unexpected risks and hazards. Many different use-cases, such as image recognition, language processing, and many others, are finding their way into the actual world. As a result, machine learning experts will have greater opportunities to shine as highly sought-after professionals.

Even though algorithms have been available for decades, their use has increased as machine learning has gained more importance. Deep learning methods are the heart of today's most advanced artificial intelligence systems. Among the most competitive areas in enterprise technology, machine learning systems are among the most popular choices, with the majority of major vendors (as well as Amazon, Google, Microsoft, IBM, and others) racing to sign up a customer for technology platforms that cover the entire spectrum of active machine learning (including data collection, data analysis, clustering techniques, model building and training), as well as application deployment and deployment of models of machine learning. It is a matter of time before the machine-learning platform wars get more intense. Machine learning started to gain importance in corporate operations, and artificial intelligence became more realistic in commercial settings. Deep learning and artificial intelligence research will continue, emphasizing generating more generic applications. Today's artificial intelligence models require much training to generate well-tuned algorithms for a certain task. However, other academics are looking at ways of making models more adaptable. They are looking for techniques enabling a machine to use context gained from one work to future distinct tasks. The amount of information generated to us is expanding all the time. For machines to learn and enhance the results and findings they give humans, they must be fed data. These outcomes may be incredibly beneficial in offering valuable insights and making educated business decisions. In recent years, machine learning has grown exponentially, and with it, the number of applications for machine learning has grown exponentially. We use machine learning throughout our daily lives more often than we realize, and we don't even realize it.

Machine learning is expected to evolve even more and assist humans more.

Chapter 7: Supervised Learning And Unsupervised Learning

2.1 Supervised Learning

As the name implies, supervised learning indicates the interaction of a supervisor who also serves as an instructor. Briefly, supervised learning would be when instructors train a computer using well-labelled data. It signifies that some report/information has already been labelled with the right answer. In supervised learning, the computer is given a fresh collection of examples (data) to analyze the training data and create an accurate result from labelled data. Consider the following scenario: you are handed a basket containing several fruits. The first stage is to teach the machine all the various fruits, as seen below.

The item will be categorized as –Apple if it has a spherical form with a dip at the top and is red.

The form of the item will be identified as – Banana if it is a long bending cylinder with a Green-Yellow tint.

Now imagine that once you've trained the data, you've given fresh independent fruit, like a banana, from the basket and requested identification.

Because the system has already learned from past data, it must utilize it intelligently this time. It will categorize the fruit based on its form and colour, validate its name as BANANA & place it in the Banana category. As a result, the machine learns from training data (a fruit basket) and then applies what it has learned to test data (new fruit).

There are 2 types of algorithms/procedures for supervised learning:

Classification: Whenever the output variable is just a category, including "Red" or "Blue," "illness", and "no disease," it is referred to as a classification issue.

Regression: A regression issue exists whenever the output variable is a real value, including "dollars" or "weight," a regression issue exists.

Supervised learning is concerned with or involves learning from "labelled" data. It signifies that some report/information has already been labelled with the right answer.

Types

Support Vector Machine

Naive Bayes Classifiers

Classification

Decision Trees

Logistic Regression

Regression

K-NN (nearest k neighbours)

Advantages

Supervised learning enables the collection of data and production of data from prior experiences.

With the assistance of experience, it is possible to optimize performance criteria.

Supervised machine learning aids in the resolution of a variety of real-world computing issues.

Disadvantages

It might not be easy to categorize copious amounts of data.

Computation time is required for supervised learning training. As a result, it brings a long time.

2.2 Unsupervised Learning

Unsupervised learning is training a computer with data that hasn't been classed or labelled and then letting the algorithm operate on that data without supervision. The machine's job here is to sort unsorted data into groups based on similarities, patterns, & differences without any previous data training. Unlike supervised learning, no instructor is present, which implies the computer will not be trained. As a result, the computer is limited in discovering hidden structures within unlabeled data. Assume it is shown a picture with both cats and dogs that it had not seen before.

As a result, the computer does not understand the characteristics of dogs and cats, and we cannot categorize/classify them as such. However, it can classify them based on their similarities, patterns, & differences, allowing us to divide the above image into two sections. The first section may have all photos with dogs, while the second half may contain all cats. You haven't learned anything yet; thus, no training data or examples exist. It enables the model to identify data and previously undetectable trends independently. It is mostly concerned with unlabeled data. There are 2 types of procedures/algorithms for unsupervised learning.

Clustering: A clustering issue is when you wish to find the data's underlying groups, such as classifying consumers based on their purchase habits.

Association: People who purchase X also tend to buy Y, for example, an association rule development issue in which you wish to identify rules that explain substantial chunks of your data.

Types

Clustering

Probabilistic

Agglomerative

Exclusive (partitioning)

Overlapping

Clustering Types

Principal Component Analysis

Hierarchical clustering

K-means clustering

Singular Value Decomposition

Independent Component Analysis

2.3 Difference between Supervised & Unsupervised Learning

Data Labelled

The key difference between the two methodologies is the usage of marked/labelled datasets. Supervised learning algorithms employ labelled input & output data, while unsupervised learning algorithms do not.

The algorithm "learns" from the education dataset by repeatedly generating predictions just on data & adjusting for the right answer in supervised learning. Although supervised learning models are more accurate than unsupervised learning methods, they need human interaction to identify the data properly. A supervised learning model, for example, can calculate/predict the length of your commute based on the time of the day, weather circumstances, & other factors. But first, one must teach it that travel time is longer in wet conditions.

Unsupervised learning models role/function independently to unearth the structure of unlabeled data. It's worth noting that confirming output variables still have to/need human interaction. A learning model which is Unsupervised, for example, may distinguish that online buyers often purchase groups of items simultaneously. However, the data analyst will

Need to confirm that grouping baby garments with a purchase of applesauce, diapers & sippy cups makes perfect sense for a recommender system.

Other significant distinctions between supervised & unsupervised learning include

Goals - The purpose of supervised learning is to anticipate new data results. You know what to anticipate from the start. An unsupervised algorithm aims to derive insights from enormous amounts of new data.

Whatever is bizarre or interesting from the dataset is governed by machine learning.

Application - Spam detection, emotion analysis, weather forecasting, and price forecasts are just a few applications/requests for supervised learning models. On the other hand, unsupervised learning is well appropriate/suited to anomaly detection, recommender systems, customer personas, and medical imaging.

Complexity - Supervised Learning algorithm is a straightforward machine learning approach usually computed using languages like R or Python. You'll need robust tools for dealing with vast unclassified data in unsupervised learning. Because they need a substantial training set to obtain the desired results, unsupervised learning methods are computationally difficult.

Drawbacks - Training supervised learning models takes time, and the labelling for input & output variables needs knowledge. Meanwhile, unsupervised learning algorithms might provide erroneous findings unless human intrusion/intervention is used to evaluate the output variables.

2.4 What's Best for You? Supervised Vs. Unsupervised Learning.

Your data scientists' assessment of the structure and amount of your data, and the use case, will determine the best method for your circumstance. Make the following considerations while making your decision

Examine the information you've provided: Is the data labelled or unlabeled? Do you have any professionals that can help with more labelling?

Chapter 8: Vectors, Matrices, Arrays

NumPy is the programming language that is the backbone of the Python deep learning stack. NumPy is a Python library that provides fast operations on data structures often used in computer vision: vectors, matrices, and tensors, among others. Even though NumPy wasn't the primary emphasis of this guide, it will appear regularly in the subsequent chapters. While working on machine learning processes, we will likely encounter many NumPy operations that we will need to learn about in this chapter.

3.1 Creating a Vector

It is necessary to generate a vector. Create the one array using NumPy by following these steps

Code

Load the library

Import numpy as np

Create a vector in the form of a row.

vector_row1 = np.array([1, 2, 3])

Create a vector in the form of a column

vector_column1 = np.array([[1],

[2],

[3]])

The multidimensional array is the primary data structure used by NumPy. The simplest way to generate a vector is to start with a one-dimensional array. These arrays, like vectors, may be represented either horizontally (in the form of rows) or vertically (in the form of columns) (i.e., columns).

3.2 Creating a Matrix

You'll need to put together a matrix. Create this double array using NumPy by following these steps:

Load the following library

import NumPy as np

Create the following matrix

matrix = np.array([[11, 22],

[11, 22],

[11, 22]])

We may utilize a NumPy multiple arrays to generate a matrix. The matrix in our approach has three rows and two columns, as shown in the diagram. NumPy offers a specific matrix data structure, which is as follows:

matrix_object = np.matrix([[11, 22],

[11, 22],

[11, 22]])

Output: Matrix1([[11, 22],

[11, 22],

[11, 22]])

On the other hand, the matrix data structure is not suggested for two reasons. The first thing to note is that arrays are the de facto standardized data structure in NumPy. Second, as previously stated, most NumPy functions return arrays rather than matrix objects.

3.3 Selecting Elements

You must choose one or more items from a vector or matrix to work with. NumPy's arrays make it simple to do so

Code

Load the library

import NumPy as np

Create a row vector

Vector_array1 = np.array([1, 12, 13, 14, 5, 6])

Create matrix

Matrix_array = np.array([[1, 2, 3],

[4, 5, 6],

[7, 8, 9]])

Choose the third element of the vector.

vector[2]

Choose the second row and the second column

matrix[1,1]

NumPy arrays, like most items in Python, are zero-indexed, which means that the value of the first element is zero, not one. NumPy provides many ways for choosing items or groupings of elements from arrays (i.e., indexes and slices). These include:

Select all elements of a vector

vector[:]

Everything up to but including the third piece should be selected.

vector[:3]

Output: array([1, 2, 3])

Everything following the third element should be selected.

vector[3:]

Output: array([4, 5, 6])

Choose the final element from the list.

vector[-1]

Output: 6

Select the first two rows, so all the columns of a grid are a starting point.

Matrix1[:2,:]

Output: array([[1, 2, 3],

[4, 5, 6]])

Select all the rows as well as the second column.

Matrix1[:,1:2]

Output: array([[2],

[5],

[8]])

3.4 Describing a Matrix

Describe the matrix's appearance by describing its form, size, and measurements.

Make use of the following terms: shape, size, or ndim:

Load the following library

import NumPy as np

Create a matrix

Matrix1 = np.array([[1, 2, 3, 4],

[5, 6, 7, 8],

[9, 10, 11, 12]])

Look at the number of columns.

Matrix1.shape

Output: (3, 4)

View elements (rows * columns)

Matrix1.size

Output: 12

View amount of dimensions

Matrix1.ndim

Output: 2

Even though this seems to be a straightforward operation (and it is), it will be useful to verify the form and size of the array regularly, both for additional computations and just as a reality check after a little operation.

3.5 Applying Operations

You wish to apply a function to several items in an array simultaneously. Make use of NumPy's vectorize function:

Load the library

import NumPy as np

Create matrix

Matrix1 = np.array([[1, 2, 3],

[4, 5, 6],

[7, 8, 9]])

Create a function that multiplies anything by 100.

addition_100 = lambda i: i + 100

Create the vectorized function of the above function

vectorized_addition_100   = np.vectorize(addition_100)

All the elements in the matrix are subjected to the function.

vectorized_addition_100(matrix)

Output: array([[101, 102, 103],

[104, 105, 106],

[107, 108, 109]])

This class turns a function into a function that can be applied to all items in an array, a slice of an array, using NumPy's vectorize method. It's important to note that vectorize is just a for loop through the items and does not result in speed

improvements. Besides that, NumPy arrays enable us to conduct operations across arrays even if their dimensions differ. For example, we can use broadcasting to produce a lot more short versions of our solution:

Increase the value of all items by 100.

matrix + 100

Output: array([[101, 102, 103],

[104, 105, 106],

[107, 108, 109]])

3.6 Finding Maximum/Minimum Values

It would help if you discovered the maximum or lowest value in the array. Make use of NumPy's maximum and minimum values:

Load library

import NumPy as np

Create the matrix

matrix1 = np.array([[1, 2, 3],

[4, 5, 6],

[7, 8, 9]])

Returning the maximum element

np.max(matrix1)

Output: 9

Returning the minimum element

np.min(matrix1)

Output: 1

We often need to understand the max and lowest values included inside an array or portion of an array. The maximum and minimum approaches may be used to achieve this. Using the axis argument, we can additionally apply the function along a specified axis:

Determine the maximum number of elements in each column.

np.maximum(matrix, axis=0)

Output: array([7, 8, 9])

Find the most significant ingredient in each row.

np.maximum(matrix, axis=1)

Output: array([3, 6, 9])

3.7 Average, Standard Deviation and Variance

You would want to compute some descriptive statistics for an array of elements. Make use of NumPy's mean, variable, and std functions:

Load the library

import NumPy as np

Create a matrix

matrix1 = np.array([[1, 2, 3],

[4, 5, 6],

[7, 8, 9]])

Return the mean of the matrix

np.mean(matrix1)

Output: 5.0

Return variance of the matrix

np.var(matrix1)

Output: 6.666666666666667

Return the standard deviation of the matrix

np.std(matrix1)

Output: 2.5819888974716112

We can easily obtain descriptive and inferential statistics about the entire matrix, or we may do computations along a particular axis in the same way that we did with max and min:

np.mean(matrix1, axis=0)

array([4.,5.,6.])

3.9 Reshaping Arrays

Suppose you wish to modify an array's form (number of columns and rows) without affecting its elements' values. Make use of NumPy's reshape function:

Code

Load the library

import NumPy as np

Create a 4x3 matrix

matrix = np.array([[1, 2, 3],

[4, 5, 6],

[7, 8, 9],

[10, 11, 12]])

Reshape the following matrix into a 2x6 matrix dimension

matrix.reshape(2, 6)

It is possible to restructure an array such that the same data is maintained but grouped in a new number of columns using the reshape function. The sole criteria are that the original and replacement matrices have the same number of items in their shapes.

In the reshape function, one handy input is -1, which indicates "as many as necessary." For example, reshape(1, -1) signifies one row and whatever number of columns are required:

matrix.reshape(1, -1)

Finally, if we input a single integer, reshape will produce a 1D array with the specified length:

matrix.reshape(12)

Chapter 9: Data Loading And Data Wrangling

To begin working on your computer vision application in Python, you must first ensure the data is properly loaded. It is important to note that CSV, comma-separated values, is the most used format for presenting machine learning data before continuing. The CSV file contains elements and features containing the machine learning information you need to know and understand. These are some examples: It is possible to automatically give names or tags to every other row of your dataset using the headers in a CSV file. It will be necessary to manually rename your attributes if your file does not have a header.

4.1 Comments

You can tell if a line in a CSV file comment has if the line begins with the hash sign (#). Depending on the technique you use to load the machine learning information, you will also have to decide whether you would like these comments to appear and how you will be able to distinguish them.

4.2 Delimiter

A delimiter is a role that divides multiple values in a column and is represented by a period (). You can use the tab (t) one more delimiter, albeit it needs to be specified in your code.

4.3 Quote

If any field values in the file include spaces, these numbers are frequently quoted, and the symbol used to indicate this is double quote marks (double quotes). If you use a separate set of characters, you must declare this in the file.

Following identifying these important components of a data file, let's learn about the various techniques for loading machine learning data into Python. To load your CSV files into Python Library, one will use the module CSV and the function reader()included in the distribution. When you load the CSV data, it will be instantly converted to a NumPy array, which can be utilized for machine learning. For example, the code below would load a dataset with no header and only numeric fields in memory when executed through the Python API. It will also convert it over to a NumPy array on its initiative.

Code

Loading a CSV file (using Python)

importing a CSV

Indians-Pima-diabetes.Data.csv is a csv file that has been imported into numpy.

raw data is equal to open(filename, 'rt') in C.

reader = csv.reader(raw data, delimiter=',', quoting=csv.QUOTE NONE); reader = csv.reader(raw data, delimiter=',', quoting=csv.QUOTE NONE);

x represents a list (reader)

numpy.array data = numpy.array (x).

astype('float')

print(data.shape)

For the uninitiated, this code instructs the program to load an object that allows iteration over every row of the data. It can be easily turned into a NumPy array. In this case, executing the code sample results in an array that has the following shape:

4.4 NumPy

Using NumPy & the numpy.loadtxt() function, you may load machine learning data into Python differently than the previous method. The function in the codebase assumes, provided your file does not contain a header row & that all the information is in the same system/format. It also presumes that the document Indians-Pima-diabetes.data.csv is in the current directory of your computer.

Code

Indians-Pima-diabetes.data.csv' is the filename to load into numpy. raw data = open(filename, 'rt') is the data to load into numpy.

```
data = numpy.loadtxt(raw data, delimiter=",")
data = numpy.loadtxt(raw data, delimiter=",")
```

```
print(data.shape)
```

4.5 Pandas

The pandas.read csv() function, available in Pandas, is the third method of loading your machine learning data. Using the pandas. Reading the CSV() function to import machine learning data is an extremely flexible and suitable approach. Upon completion, it delivers pandas.DataFrame, allows you to begin summarising and graphing data instantly. The code sample provided below imagines/assumes that now the Indians-Pima-diabetes.data.csv document is in the current directory of the computer's hard drive.

Code

```python
import pandas as pd
```

Set the filename and column names

```python
filename = 'Indians-Pima-diabetes.Data.csv'

names = ['preg', 'plas', 'pres', 'skin', 'test', 'mass', 'pedi', 'age', 'class']
```

Load the CSV file into a pandas dataframe

```python
data = pd.read_csv(filename, names=names)
```

Print the shape of the dataframe

```python
print(data.shape)
```

4.6 Data Wrangling

It is also known as data munging when it changes and maps data from one "raw" data type into another to make it more acceptable and valuable for many downstream uses such as analytics. Data wrangling aims to ensure that the data is high quality and useful.

When it comes to data analysis, data analysts usually spend most of their time, for example, on data wrangling rather than conducting the analysis. Further munging, data visualization, data aggregation, retraining a statistical model, and various other potential applications are all possible during data wrangling. A typical data wrangling process consists of a series of general processes that begin with obtaining the data in its raw form from the source data, "munging" processing raw data (by sorting it or parsing it), and lastly, depositing the generated content into a base station for storage and later use. Data wrangling is a method that is used when creating an interactive model, and it is conducted during this process. In another way, it's being used to convert raw data into a more convenient format for data consumers to consume. This approach is referred to as Data Munging in some circles. After collecting data from various sources, certain algorithms are used to sort the data. Then the data is decomposed into a new structured format before being stored in another database. Data wrangling is a critical component in inputting the model into action. As a result, information is transferred to the most practical format possible before any model can be applied. It will likely improve the model's accuracy by filtration, grouping, and picking suitable data sets. Another concept is that, when dealing with time-series data, each algorithm is performed with a distinct set of parameters depending on the situation. As a result, Data Wrangling is employed to convert the data over the period into the format required by the applied modelling model. In plain language, the dense data is translated into a format that can be used for further investigation and analysis.

What are the advantages of using Data Wrangling?

When adopting Deep Learning and Deep Learning, Data Wrangling is utilized to address the issue of Information Leaks. Primarily, we must comprehend what Data Leakage is.

4.7 Data leakage

Data Leakage is accountable for the emergence of an invalid Evolutionary

Computation Learning model because of the over-optimization of the model that has been implemented.

When data from outside, i.e., data that is not present in the training dataset, is used by the educational process of the model, this is referred to as data leakage, and it is defined as follows: According to the applied model, this research. The knowledge objectives will cause the model's calculated expected performance to be less than satisfactory. For example, if we wish to use a specific feature for Predictive Analysis, that special part is not present when the dataset is being trained. Stolen data will just be introduced into the model. Stolen data can be proved in a variety of methods, some of which are listed below:

Data may leak from the test dataset toward the training data. Amplification of the error in the computed predicted outcome to the training sample. There is a leakage of the new dataset into previous data. The use of data outside the purview of the algorithm being used. Data leakage from two major contributors to Learning Algorithms and Learning techniques, namely feature characteristics (variables) and the training data set, has been reported recently. Checking for the presence or Data Leakage inside the model under consideration. When complicated datasets are used, it is common to see data leakage. When separating a time series database into training and testing sets, the data is a complicated task to solve.

Implementing sampling in such a graphical issue is time-consuming and difficult. Keeping track of analogue observations in the form of audio recordings and photos in separate files with a fixed size and timestamp.

Chapter 10: Dataset Preparation

A specialized data scientist must prepare all data if you're thinking about a spherical machine-learning cow. And that's about correct. You don't have machine learning if you don't have a data analyst on board to conduct all the cleaning. However, firms that cannot afford data science staff must attempt to convert current IT experts into the discipline. Furthermore, dataset preparation is not limited to the skills of a data scientist. How an organization is constructed, procedures developed, and whether the personnel follows instructions in recordkeeping may cause issues with machine learning datasets. You may depend on a data scientist for dataset preparation. Still, there is a way to effectively ease the burden of the person facing this extraordinary work by understanding some approaches in advance. Let's look at some of the most prevalent dataset issues and how to fix them.

5.1 What to Do If You Don't Have Any Data For Machine Learning?

Years of data collection have built a boundary between individuals who can dabble with Machine Learning and those who can't. Some businesses have been stockpiling records for generations with a such tremendous success that they now need

trucks to transport them to the cloud since traditional bandwidth is insufficient.

Lack of information is anticipated for individuals new to the scene, but there are methods to transform that drawback into a positive.

To begin ML execution, start with open-source datasets. Plenty of data is available for machine learning, and some firms (such as Google) are willing to provide it. Later, we'll discuss the benefits of using public datasets. While such chances exist, the true value comes from golden data morsels mined from your company's business choices and operations.

Second, and unsurprisingly, you now could correctly gather data. Companies that began collecting data with paper ledgers & ended up with.xlsx and.csv files will have a tougher difficulty preparing data than those with a tiny but proud Machine Learning-friendly dataset. You can customize a data-gathering method in advance if you know the objectives that deep learning should tackle.

What about huge data, for example? It's so popular that it is the thing that everybody is doing. It's a good mentality to start with large data in mind, but big data isn't about petabytes. It's all about being able to process them correctly. The more data you have, the more difficult it is to derive insights. Just because you have a lot of timber doesn't mean you can turn it into a garage full of tables and chairs. As a result, the common advice for newcomers is to start modestly and simplify their data.

5.2 Articulate Problem Early

Knowing whatever you want to forecast can assist you in determining which data is more beneficial to gather. Conduct data exploration & attempt to think in the areas of classification, regression, clustering, and ranking that we discussed in our whitepaper on commercial applying machine learning when formulating the challenge. These duties are differentiated in the come-out of fashion in informal language:

Classification - You need an algorithm that answers binaries of yes-or-no questions (cats vs dogs, good vs evil, sheep vs goats, etc.) or a multiclass categorization (grass, bushes or trees, cats, birds, or dogs etc.) You'll also need to annotate the correct answers so that an algorithm may learn from them.

Clustering - You're looking for an algorithm to determine the categorization criteria and the number of pieces of training. The primary argument between this & classification jobs is that you don't know the categories & division principles. It is common, for example, when you need to separate your consumers & customize a distinctive approach to each section based on its characteristics.

Regression - You would like an algorithm to produce a numerical value. For example, suppose businesses spend too long figuring out the proper evaluation for your product because it relies on so many variable stars. In that case, regression techniques may help you estimate it.

Ranking - Some ml algorithms rank objects based on characteristics. The ranking often suggests movies in video services or displays things a consumer is likely to buy based on previous search and purchase actions.This basic segmentation will address your business challenge, and you may begin altering a dataset appropriately. At this level, the thumb rule is to avoid too intricate issues.

5.3 Data Collection Mechanisms

Creating an information culture in a business is the most difficult aspect of the project. We touched on this briefly in our piece on the machine-learning approach. The first step in using machine learning for predictive analytics is eliminating data fragmentation. For example, data dispersion is among the main analytics concerns in travel technology, one of AltexSoft's major areas of competence. The hotel divisions in charge of fundamental characteristics get personal information about their clients. Hotels can access visitors' credit card details, preferred amenities, home addresses, guest services use, and even beverages and meals bought during their stay. Various departments, and even different monitoring points within a department, have their silos of data. Marketers may well have exposure to a CRM, but the clients in that database are not linked to web analytics. If you have a lot of channels for engagement, acquisition, & retention, it's not always viable to consolidate all streams of data into a single store, but it's usually doable.

A data engineer, a professional responsible for establishing data infrastructures, usually gathers data. However, you may hire a software engineer with database skills in the early phases. Data-gathering systems may be divided into two categories.

Data Warehouses & ETL

The first is data storage in warehouses. Structural (or SQL) records, which fit into conventional table forms, are often stored in these storages. All your record sales, payroll, and CRM data will likely fall into this group. Transforming data before putting it into a warehouse is another conventional aspect of dealing with warehouses. The techniques for data transformation will be discussed in further depth in this book. However, you must know whatever data you want and how it should be presented so you examine everything before storing it. Extract, Transform, and Load is the name of this technique (ETL).

The dilemma/crisis with this approach is that you don't know which data will be useful and which will be useless. Consequently, warehouses often present the metrics that business intelligence interfaces know they need to track. There's a third choice as well.

Data Lakes & ELT

The Data Lake is a storage system that can store both structured & unstructured data, such as photographs, videos, voice recordings, PDF files, etc. Even though data is arranged, it is not changed before being saved. You would import data in its present condition and then decide how to use and treat it as needed. Extract, Load, and Save (ELS) is the name of this procedure, & — when needed — Transform. This essay goes through the differences between ETL & ELT in further detail. So, which option should you take? Both, in most cases. Machine learning is said to be more suited to data lakes. However, if you have confidence in, at minimum, some data, it's good having it on hand so you may utilize it for analyses before embarking on a data science project.

Chapter 11: Model Selection And Model Evaluation

Many alternative machine learning models may be fitted to a given predictive modelling dataset using simple machine learning libraries such as sci-kit-learn and Keras, available for free download. Therefore, the issue of machine learning becomes determining which models are appropriate for your situation from among many available options.

You could assume that the model's performance is adequate. Still, it would help if you considered additional factors, such as how long it takes to train the model and how straightforward it is to communicate to project stakeholders before proceeding. Their problems become much more serious if the selected model must be employed in an operational capacity for many months or years.

What precisely are you selecting: only the method used to fit a model, or the complete data preparation and model fitting workflow, for example?

Machine Learning is the marriage of statistics and computing at its most basic level. The heart of machine learning is the idea of algorithms or models, essentially statistical guesses taken to the next level of sophistication.

Each model, however, has several constraints dependent on the data dispersion used to construct it. Because they are just estimates, none can be relied upon to be completely correct (even if on steroids). Bias and variance are two terms often used to describe these limits. A model with high bias will overstate by paying less attention to the examples. The generalization ability with high variance is limited to the training data. It will not generalize to test points it has never seen (for example, Random Forests with max depth = None).

When there are only minor restrictions, such as when we must pick between a random forest approach and a gradient boosting technique or when we must choose between two variants of the same decision tree algorithm, the problem emerges. Both will have a large variance and a low bias in most cases.

Model assessment is a technique for determining whether models are accurate based on test results. The test data comprises data items that the model has never previously observed.

It is a strategy for picking the best model once all the individual models have been assessed based on the necessary criteria.

Model selection is a process of picking one ultimate machine learning model to choose among a group of prospective machine learning for use with a training dataset from among a library of applicant machine learning

Model selection refers to the process applied across different models and models of the same type defined with various model hyperparameters. It can be implemented across different models and designs of the same type equipped with various model hyperparameters.

In the case of a dataset, we could be interested in constructing a classification and regression problems prediction model for that data set. It is impossible to predict which solution will perform the best on this task in advance since it is unknown. For this reason, we develop and assess various potential models for the issue.

Model evaluation is the process of assessing the performance of a model, while model selection determines the appropriate degree of leeway for a model to use.

6.1 Considerations of Model Selection

Considering the statistical random noise and the incompleteness of the data sample, and the limits of each model type, it is reasonable to expect some predicted inaccuracy from all models. As a result, the idea of an ideal or ideal model is no longer relevant. As a substitute, we must look for a " good enough model."

Specific criteria, such as supportability and a restricted level of model complexity, may be specified by project stakeholders. As a result, choosing a model that requires less ability but is easier and simpler to grasp may be preferable.

Alternatively, suppose model competence is more important than all other considerations. In that case, the ability of a model to function well on the data will be favoured regardless of the level of computing complexity required.

Consequently, a "good enough" model may relate to many different things and can be tailored to your project, such as:

Develop a model that fulfils the needs and limits of project stakeholders.

An adequately skilled simulation in the time and budget constraints available for development.

a simulation that is more skilled as compared to more nave models

A model that performs well compared to other models that have been evaluated.

A model that performs well compared to the current state of the art.

Following that, we must examine the items that have been chosen.

For example, we aren't picking a best-fit model since all models would be eliminated regardless of fit. It is because, after we have selected a model, you will fit a perfect revised model to all the existing data and begin using it to forecast the future.

As a result, are we choosing between the methods to fit the model to the training dataset?

Some methods need data planning to provide the learning algorithm with the most accurate representation of the problem's structure. Consequently, we must go another step and consider model selection to be picking among model creation pipelines rather than just selecting among models.

Even though each pipeline takes in the same input training dataset and produces a model that can be assessed in the same way, each pipeline may need separate or overlapping computing processes, such as data filtering:

Selection of characteristics.

Feature manufacturing is the method of creating brand-new features.

The more closely you examine the model selection problem, the more subtlety you see. Having been acquainted with some of the factors that should be considered when picking a model.

6.2 Model Selection Techniques

The most effective method to model selection necessitates collecting "enough" data, which might be almost endless depending on the situation's complexity. If we were in an ideal situation, folks would divide the data into training, validation, and test data. We would then fit applicant models just on training data, evaluate and select the best models on the validation data, and finally report the outcome of the overall model just on test data.

The optimum strategy for dealing with a large amount of data is to randomly partition the dataset into 3 categories: a training set, validation set, and test set, as shown in the figure.

It is unworkable for most predictive modelling issues because we seldom have enough data or who can determine what data would be adequate.

We recognize that the amount of data available for training and validation will be restricted in many applications. We want to utilize as much available information as possible for the training phase to develop strong models. Nevertheless, if the validation data is limited, the estimate of prediction accuracy will be erratic and noisy as a result.

6.3 Types of Model Selection

1. Resampling Methods

As the name implies, resampling methods are straightforward ways of rearranging data samples to determine whether a model works well on sample data that have not been trained on. In other terms, resampling allows us to determine whether a model will generalize well.

2. Random Split

It is possible to randomly select a proportion of data into learning, testing, and, ideally, validation sets by using Random Splits in R. The benefit of using this strategy is there is a fair possibility that the native inhabitants will be well reflected in all three sets of data collected. In more technical terms, randomized splitting will prevent data from being sampled in a biassed manner.

The validation data is the second set, and it is reasonable to wonder why there are two test sets.

The testing set evaluates the model's performance when selecting features and model tweaking. It implies that the model and feature set parameters are chosen to provide the best possible result on the test set. As a result, the validation set, which contains data points that have never been seen before (since they were not utilized in the tune and feature-based modules), is used for the final assessment.

3. Time-Based Split

In certain cases, random splits aren't feasible due to the nature of the data. To train a system for weather prediction, we cannot split the train and test sets at random, as we would in other situations. It will cause the seasonal rhythm to get jumbled! Time Series data is a word that is often used to describe this kind of information.

In such instances, a time-based split is implemented. The training set may include data from the previous three years and the first ten months of the current year. The last two months

might be left aside for testing and validation of the final product.

There is also the idea of window sets, in which the model learns till a certain date and is then tested on subsequent dates iteratively, with the training window growing by one day each time the model is evaluated. Whenever the test set is small, the benefit of this strategy is that it stabilizes the model and avoids overfitting, which is beneficial.

On the other hand, the disadvantage of time-series data is that the occurrences or statistics are not independent. A single occurrence might impact every data entry that occurs after it.

An election result that results in a change in the ruling party, for example, might have a significant impact on the population statistics in the following years. Alternatively, the notorious coronavirus epidemic will significantly influence economic statistics over the following several years.

In this situation, no deep learning model was trained on previous data since the data points collected during the occurrence are significantly different.

4. Cross-Validation K-Fold

The cross-validation approach works by randomly shuffling

the dataset and dividing it into k groups of equal size and complexity. After iterating over each grouping, the group must be treated as a test set, while all other groups must be combined to form the training set, and so on. The model has been tested just on the test group, and the procedure is repeated for a total of k groups of participants.

It results in k separate test groups yielding k different outcomes after the procedure. The most suitable model may then be picked relatively easily by selecting the model with the best score.

5. Bootstrap

Obtaining a stable model using Bootstrap is among the most powerful methods available. As a result, it is like the randomized splitting approach in that it is based on the notion of random sampling.

The first task is to decide the appropriate sample size. A random sample data point from the original data must be picked and included in the bootstrap sample. Immediately after the addition, each sample must be reinserted into the initial image. This method must be done N times, wherein N is the number of samples to be examined.

Chapter 12: Algorithms Chains And Pipelines

Most individuals know that machine learning generates value, but few know how it does so. When does value creation begin, and when does it end? Contrary to popular assumptions, developing algorithms is just a minor part. Following pathways in the nearest neighbour graphs of the clusters, the algorithm's central concept is to locate pairs of clusters that should be merged. In the end, every such path would eventually lead to a couple of clusters that are the closest neighbours to one another, and the algorithm selects that pair of clusters also as pair that will be merged. A stacking data structure records each route the algorithm follows, saving time by reusing as much of each path as feasible. It saves time by allowing the algorithm to reuse as much of each path as possible.

The nearest-neighbour chained algorithm combines clusters inside a different sequence than approaches that always discover and merge the first closest pair of clusters. It is accomplished by following pathways in this manner. Despite this, it always constructs the same set of clusters, regardless of the change in the input data. Machine learning techniques can be implemented in the Industrial Internet of Things to enjoy the benefits of cost reductions, better time efficiency, and improved performance. In the recent past, we have all benefited from machine learning techniques, whether from streaming movie companies that recommend titles you watch based on reading habits or from financial institutions that monitor illegal transactions based on the spending patterns of consumers. It can process big and complex data sets to uncover intriguing patterns or trends, such as anomalies. Machines must digest information quickly and make choices before reaching a certain importance threshold.

7.1 Machine Learning's Value Chain

A value chain represents the series of operations through which corporations add importance to a product from start to finish. Traditional industries have a straightforward value chain. Selling fresh buns is the last step in your neighbourhood bakery's long chain of activities: raw material procurement, supply chain, storage, cooking, sales, and distribution. On the other hand, what are the many value-adding tasks of machine learning? Contrary to popular opinion, algorithm programming is only a small portion of the overall ML value chain. Other value-adding procedures take place during the ML programming.

Machine Learning may be a useful tool for a variety of jobs. On the other hand, understanding the problem, identifying goals, and sketching a plan of action are not easy tasks. Clearly describe the business goals you want to achieve with an ML solution before considering how to apply it. Set up checkpoints along the road so that you can track your progress.

149

Knowing and understanding the present solution and the specific steps where machine learning could help. Consider the persons involved. What will be their reactions to the new solution?

There are six important steps in the ML value chain:

Data Gathering

Data collection is the process of acquiring raw data. It's a crucial stage because machine learning normally necessitates large data. It is mostly true in the briefcase of deep learning, a machine learning branch. Deep learning algorithms typically require hundreds, if not millions, of data sets to learn. External data includes publicly available datasets, such as those found through Google's Sets of Search Engines and data that may be bought or scraped off the internet. Due to a lack of internal data and the high expenses of obtaining external data, some businesses turn to a third option: collaborating with other businesses to pool their data, sometimes even with competitors.

Storage Of Data

Once the data has remained collected, it must be stored in a secure location: The process of assembling raw data in the data centres is known as data storage. Because machine learning involves such a large amount of data, storage capacity is an essential component of the entire value chain. Most firms used to store information according to their servers in the early days of machine learning - not ideal. Data can now be saved and accessible at speeds and low cost, thanks to the growth of cloud technology, and some programs, such as Levity, include storage as a standard feature at no extra cost.

Chapter 13: Decision Trees

Decision Trees (DTs) are a quasi-supervised learning approach for classification & regression. The intention/objective is to learn basic decision rules from data attributes to develop a model that can predict/foresee the value of the dependent variable. A tree approximates a piecewise constant.

In the instance below, decision trees use a succession/series of if decision rules to approximate a sine curve using data. Decision criteria get more complicated as the tree grows deeper and the model becomes more accurate.

Decision trees provide the following advantages:

Easy to comprehend and apply. Visualizing trees is possible.

Data preparation is minimal. Data normalization, dummy variables, and removing blank entries are all common requirements for other procedures. However, missing values are not supported by this module.

The cost of utilizing the tree (predicting data) is proportional to the number of data points needed to train it.

Has the ability to work with both numerical & categorical data. For now, however, the sci-kit-learn implementation does not support categorical variables. Other methods are often used to analyze datasets with just one kind of variable. For additional details, see Algorithms.

Capable of dealing with situations with many outputs

This model is based on a white box. If a scene can be seen in a model, Boolean logic may be used to describe it. In contrast, a black box design (such as a deep neural network) are more difficult to decipher.

Statistical tests may be used to verify a model's accuracy. As a result, the model's dependability may be taken into consideration.

Works effectively even when the real model used to create the data violates certain assumptions.

Decision trees have the following drawbacks:

Decision-tree learners may produce too thorny trees that fail to generalize data effectively. Overfitting is the term for this kind of behaviour. To overcome this issue, mechanisms like pruning, limiting the number of samples needed at each leaf node, and limiting the tree's maximum depth are required.

Decision trees are inherently unstable since slight changes in the data may create an entirely new tree. Using decision trees as part of an ensemble, this issue is reduced.

Decision tree predictions are piecewise constant approximations, as seen in the diagram above, rather than smooth or continuous predictions. As a result, extrapolation is a problem for them.

It is well known that learning an optimum decision tree is NP-complete for numerous features of optimality & even for basic notions.

As a result, practical decision-tree machine learning uses heuristic algorithms like the greedy algorithm, making locally optimum judgments at each node. These algorithms can't assure/promise that they'll yield the best decision tree. It may be precluded by using a collective/ensemble learner to train numerous trees, with the features & samples being selected randomly with replacement.

Some topics, like XOR, parity, and multiplexer difficulties, are difficult to grasp since decision trees need not represent them.

If certain classes dominate, decision-tree learners produce little trees. Before matching with the decision tree, the dataset is advised to be balanced.

8.1 Classification

A Decision Tree Classifier is a class capable of multi-class categorization on a dataset. Like other classifiers, it accepts two arrays as input: a sparse or dense array X of the form (n samples, n features) containing the training data and an array

Y of decimal numbers of shape (n samples, n labels) containing the classifier for the training images.

8.2 Problems Multi-output

When Y is a 2d array of the form (n samples, n outputs), a multi-output question is a supervised training problem with multiple outputs to predict.

Since there is no connection between the outputs, a straightforward solution is to create n separate models, one per output, and then use those forecasting methods for each of the n outputs individually. However, since the output values associated with the same input are likely to be correlated, it is preferable to create a single model able to accurately predict all n outputs simultaneously. First, it takes less time to train since just one estimator is created. Second, the resultant estimator's generalization accuracy may often be improved.

This method works well for multi-output situations when it comes to decision trees. It necessitates the following modifications:

Instead of one, hold n simulation results in leaves.

Calculate the average decrease throughout all n outputs using splitting criteria.

This module supports multi-output situations by implementing this method in Decision Tree Classifier and Regressor. Whenever the decision tree is fitted to an output array Y of the form (n samples, n outputs), the estimator produced is:

On predict, output n output values.

On predict proba, return a list of n output array of class probabilities.

Multi-output Tree-Based Regression demonstrates the usage of inter-trees for regression. The input X in this example is still a real number, and output Y is X's sine and cosine.

Face completion with multi-output estimators demonstrates the usage of cross trees for classification. The images of the top half of the faces are inputs X, and the pixels of the bottom half of those faces are outputs Y in this example.

8.3 Complexity

In general, the time it takes to build a balanced tree structure is O(nsamplesnfeatureslog (nsamples)), and the time it takes to query it is O(log(nsamples)). Although the tree-building algorithm strives to create balanced trees, this is not always true. Assuming that the subtrees are balanced, the price at each node is determined by searching through O(nfeatures) for the feature that reduces entropy the most. At each node, the cost is O(nfeaturesnsampleslog (nsamples)), resulting in a total cost of O(nfeaturesnsamples2log(nsamples) for the whole tree (by adding the costs at each node).

8.4 Practical Use Suggestions

On information with a high number of characteristics, decision trees tend to overfit. Having the proper sample-to-feature ratio is crucial since a tree with few samples in a high-dimensional space is extremely prone to overfitting.

Perform dimensionality reduction beforehand to improve your tree's chances of identifying discriminative features.

Grasp the decision configuration will aid in acquiring a better understanding of how the decision tree produces predictions, which is crucial for comprehending the data's key properties.

Use the export tool to see the tree as you train. To understand how the tree adapts to your data, start with max depth=3 and gradually raise the depth.

Remember that the number of examples necessary to fill the tree doubles for each new level the tree reaches. To avoid overfitting, use max depth to limit the tree size.

Control which divides will be examined using min samples split or min samples leaf to guarantee that many samples influence every choice in the tree. A small value indicates that the tree will significantly outperform the data, while a substantial number indicates that the tree will not learn the data. As a starting point, try min samples leaf=5. If the sample size fluctuates substantially, an afloat value may be utilized as a percentage within those two parameters. While min samples split may make any number of little leaves, min samples leaf ensures that each leaf does have a minimum size, preventing low-variance, excessive leaf nodes in extrapolation situations. Min samples leaf=1 is frequently the best option for segmentation with few classes.

If sample weight is specified, min samples split evaluates samples directly and independently of the sample weight. If you need to account for sample weights at splits, use min weight fraction leaf or min impurity decrease.

Before training, balance your dataset to avoid the tree from being skewed toward dominating classes. Class balancing may be accomplished by taking an equal sample size from each classroom or converting each class's sum of example weights to a single value. Also, weight-based pre-pruning criteria like min weight fraction leaf will be less biased toward dominant classes than criteria like min samples leaf, which are unaware of sample weights.

If the samples are weighted using weight-based pre-pruning criteria like min weight fraction leaf, which ensures that leaf nodes contain a minimum fraction of the total sum of the sample weights, it will be simpler to optimize the tree structure.

Internally, all decision trees employ np.float32 arrays. A dataset copy will be created if the training data isn't in this format.

If input matrix X is sparse, use sparse csc matrix before using fit & sparse csr matrix before applying predict. When attributes are null in most samples, training time for a scant matrix input may be magnitudes quicker than for a dense matrix.

Chapter 14: Naive Bayes

The Naive Bayes algorithm is a learning technique based on the Bayes theorem to solve computer science classification issues. It is mostly used in text categorization that needs many training data points.

The Naive Bayes Classifier is among the most simple and successful Classification algorithms available. It aids in developing rapid machine learning that can produce accurate predictions in a brief period. Spam filtering, sentiment analysis, and article classification are widely used applications of the Naive Bayes Algorithm.

The Naive Bayes algorithm is made from the terms Nave and Bayes, which may be stated in the following manner:

Naive: It is so named because it is predicated on the assumption that the existence of a certain characteristic is unrelated to the occurrence of any other features. For example, if the apple is recognized as an apple based on its colour, shape, and flavour, then a red, round, and delicious fruit is recognized as a fruit of the apple family. As a result, each characteristic contributes to identifying an apple without relying on the other characteristics.

Bayes: The term "Bayes" refers to the fact that it is based on the premise of Bayes' Theorem. The conditional probability has an impact on this.

According to Bayes' theorem, the following is the formula

In this case, P(A|B) is the probability of future occurrence: Hypothesis A's influence on observed occurrence B is represented by the probability of assumption A.

P(B|A) is the product of two variables. Probability of occurrence (likelihood): Probability of evidence presented that the likelihood of a hypothesis being true is true.

Prior Probability (P (A)) is the probability of a hypothesis being correct before viewing the evidence.

P(B) denotes Marginal Probability: the probability of a given event occurring.

9.1 Working of Naïve Bayes

It is easier to understand how the Nave Bayes Classifier works if you consider the following example:

Consider the following scenario: we have such data of weather and an associated goal variable called "Play." As a result, we

Must use this information to determine whether we should play on a specific day based on the weather circumstances. So, to resolve this issue, we must follow the procedures outlined below:

Convert the supplied dataset into frequency distribution tables using the following formula.

Create a Likelihood table by calculating the probabilities of the attributes that have been provided.

Calculate the prior distribution using Bayes's theorem at this point.

Advantages of the Naive Bayes Classifier:

Naive Bayes is a quick and simple machine-learning method for predicting a data class.

It may be used for binary and multi-class classifications depending on the situation.

When compared to other Algorithms, it does very well in multi-class predictions.

In the case of text categorization issues, this is the most often used algorithm.

Disadvantages of the Naive Bayes Classifier:

Because the Naive Bayes algorithm believes that all characteristics are independent or unconnected, it cannot learn the link between them.

Chapter 15: The Clustering Technique

It is essential in the unsupervised learning approach in its most basic form. In an unsupervised learning method, we pull references from data consisting of input data but no labelled answers, which we then use to train our models. In general, it is used to discover lengthwise, underlying explanatory mechanisms, generative properties, and groupings inherent in a collection of instances, among other things. Data clustering is the challenge of dividing a population or a set of data items into various groups so that data entries in the same groupings are more likely to be confident in the same group and more dissimilar to data points in diverse groups. It is a group of nodes based on their similarities and differences. The data points in therein graph below can be categorized into a single category based on their characteristics. We can tell the difference between the cluster, and we can tell that there are three clusters in the photo below.

DBSCAN is an acronym for Density-based Spatial Cluster of Applications with Noise. These pieces of information are grouped based on the fundamental premise that the data source lies within a specific constraint of distance from the cluster's centre. A variety of distance methodologies and approaches are employed to calculate the outliers.

10.1 What Is The Purpose Of Clustering?

As previously said, Clustering is quite significant because it provides the intrinsic group among the existing unlabeled data. There are no established criteria for effective Clustering. It is up to the user to determine what criteria they will use to determine whether their requirement has been met. Consider the following examples: finding representative data objects for homogeneous groups (regression analysis), discovering "natural clusters" and describing their unknown properties ("natural" data types), discovering useful and appropriate groupings ("useful" data classes) or discovering unusual data objects (data exploration) (outlier detection). This technique must make various assumptions about the similarity of points, and each assumption results in a different but equally valid cluster formation.

10.2 Methods Of Clustering Classification

Hard Clustering and Soft Clustering are the two main types of clustering methods. However, there are various additional ways of Clustering that can be used. The following are the most often-used clustering approaches in machine learning:

Partitioning and Clustering are the first two steps.

The second method is called Density-Based Clustering.

3. Clustering based on Distribution Models

4. Hierarchical Clustering (also known as hierarchical Clustering)

5. Fuzzy Clustering (also known as fuzzy Clustering)

Partitioning and Clustering are two terms used to describe dividing and combining things. It is a Clustering in which the data is divided into groups that are not hierarchical. The centroid-based method is another name for this technique.

The K-Means Clustering technique is the most encountered example of partitioning clustering.In this type, the dataset is separated into k groups, where K is the number of pre-defined groups and is the number of groups in the dataset. The cluster centre is constructed so that the remoteness between data points in one cluster and the centroid of another cluster is kept to a bare minimum compared to another cluster centroid. Density-Based Clustering is a type of Clustering that is based on density. Using the density-based clustering method, highly dense areas are connected to form clusters, and arbitrarily shaped allocations are formed if the dark region can be connected to form the clusters. This method accomplishes this by finding different clusters in the dataset and connecting the areas with high density into larger clusters of similar clusters. The sparser parts of data space separate the dense sections of data space. When dealing with a dataset with varied densities and large dimensions, these techniques may have difficulties grouping the data points. Clustering based on Distribution Models. For example, in the distributions model-based clustering method, datasets are separated according to how likely each dataset belongs to a given distribution. The grouping is accomplished by assuming certain distributions, typically the Gaussian Distribution. The Expectation-The Maximization Clustering algorithm, which uses Gaussian Mixture Models, is an example of this type of algorithm (GMM).

10.3 Clustering in a Hierarchical Structure

Because there is no obligation to define the clusters to be produced in advance, the clustering method can be utilized as an alternative to partitioned Clustering. As a result of this approach, the dataset is separated into clusters, which are then combined to form a tree-like architecture, also known as a dendrogram. By slicing the trees at the appropriate level, selecting either a single observation or cluster centres is possible. An example of this system is the Hierarchical Agglomerative algorithm, the most often used in computer science. Fuzzy Clustering is a type of Clustering that is based on fuzzy logic. Clustering is a soft approach in which a piece of data can be assigned to more than just a group or cluster simultaneously. Each dataset contains a set of participation coefficients proportional to how a dataset is a cluster member. Among the algorithms/procedures that fall into this category is the Fuzzy C-means algorithm, referred to as the Fuzz k-means algorithm in some circles.

10.4 Algorithms for Clustering

The Clusters algorithms can be classified based on the previously discussed models.

Many ways of categorizing algorithms have been described, but only a few are still widely employed. The clustering algorithm we apply depends on the data type we are working with. Among other things, some algorithms are required to guess the clustering algorithm in the given dataset. In contrast, others are required to discover the shortest distance between the observations in the supplied dataset.

Specifically, we will explore the following popular Clustering methods that are commonly employed in machine learning:

The K-Means algorithm (also known as the K-means clustering algorithm): The k-means method is one of the market's most widely used clustering algorithms today. It categorizes the

Dataset by separating the samples into clusters with identical variances, which are then classified. For this technique to work, the centroids must be given. It is fast because it requires fewer computations and only has a linear O. (n) complexity.

Mean-shift algorithm: The method attempts to discover dense spots in a smooth density among data points by shifting the data points around. It is an instance of a clustering model concerned with updating all candidates for Centro to be the centre of the points inside a particular region to maximize accuracy.

DBSCAN Algorithm (Deep Blue Scanner): Spatial Concentration Clustering of Apps in Noise is the abbreviation for this technique. Although it is like the mean-shift model, it has some notable advantages over density-based modelling. This technique separates the densely populated areas from the less densely populated areas. As a result, the clusters might be found in various shapes that are completely random. Expectation-Maximization GMM clustering is used in the following situations: This algorithm will be used as a substitute for such k-means algorithm or when the k-means algorithm

174

cannot be applied. In GMM, the real numbers are expected to be distributed Gaussian. Agglomerative Hierarchy Algorithm: The bottom-up hierarchical clustering algorithm clusters data. Each data point is regarded as a single cluster at the outset, and then the clusters are gradually blended. An example of a tree-structure representation of the cluster hierarchy is shown below. Affinity Propagation: This clustering technique differs from previous clustering algorithms in that it does not require the user to identify the number of nodes to be created. In this case, each data point communicates with the next data point in the pair until convergence is reached. The algorithm's primary disadvantage is its O(N2T) computation time.

10.5 Clustering Has A Variety Of Applications

The following are some examples of well-known applications of the clustering approach in Machine Learning: When it comes to cancer cell identification, clustering algorithms are commonly utilized. For example, when it comes to the identification of malignant cells. Cancerous & non-cancerous data sets are separated into diverse groups by this method. Clustering is also used in search engines, which means that search engines also use the technique. The quest result is based on the object closest to the search engine. Identifying common data objects together in a group geographically separated from the other different objects accomplishes this. The quality of the clustering method determines how accurate the result of such a query is. Marketing researchers employ customer segmentation to categorize and categorize customers according to their choices and preferences.

Chapter 16: Practices For Hyperparameter Tuning

When choosing the correct deep/ model of machine learning and increasing the model's performance, every ML Engineer & Data Scientist must recognize the significance of "Hyperparameter Tuning (HPs-T)" (s).

In other words, selecting a machine learning model is a huge undertaking entirely dependent on choosing equivalent hyper-parameters, all required to train a model. It always refers to the parameters of a chosen model, which cannot be learned from data and must be delivered before the model enters the training stage. The model of machine learning's performance advances with a better option of hyperparameter tuning & selection procedures. This paper's central/main goal is to raise awareness of hyperparameter tuning. Tweaking the model's parameters is called hyperparameter tuning, and it is a time-consuming operation. Before we go into the particulars, let's ask ourselves some important questions about hyperparameter tuning. I'm sure this will assist you a lot with this vague term. That is something I have personally experienced and will describe here.

11.1 What are Hyperparameters?

As we all know, some parameters are internally learned and derived from a dataset and used to make predictions, classifications, and so on. These are known as Model Parameters, & they vary depending on the data type. We can't control this because it is dependent on the data. The value of indices learned from the given dataset is represented by the letters'm' and 'C' in a linear equation. Hyperparameters are a set of parameters that govern the behaviour of a model/algorithm and are adaptable to produce an improved model with optimal performance.

11.2 Why Is Hyperparameter Tuning Important in Machine Learning?

Models of machine learning ls aren't smart enough to determine which hyperparameters will result in the best accuracy on a given dataset. However, when hyperparameter values are set correctly, they can help develop extremely accurate models; therefore, we let our models experiment with multiple hyperparameter combinations during the training process and generate predictions using the optimal configuration of hyperparameter values. n estimators, max depth (depth of each tree in the forest), & criterion are some of the hyperparameters within the Random Forest Classifier. Setting n estimators to 1 or 2 makes no sense because a forest has much more trees, but how can we determine what number of plants will produce the best results? We experiment with values such as [100, 200, 300]. We can readily find the optimal number of trees in the forest because the model will test all three given numbers.

11.3 Hyperparameter Tuning in Python

Random search, Grid search & Informed search are the three hyperparameter tuning methods in Python. Let's take a closer look at them.

Search Grid

As the image above shows, a grid is a series of squares and rectangles formed by intersecting lines. Every square in a grid has a separate set of hyperparameters within grid search, and the model must learn each one. Assume we wish to train the Random Forest Algorithm with the following units of hyperparameters for a better understanding.

[100, 150, 200] n estimators

[20, 30, 40] max depth

Look at the grid that these hyperparameter values have created. Our model conducts training on each permutation of n estimators and max depth.

11.4 Randomized Search in Python is Implemented.

Lines 1 and 2 import random search & describe our model, Random Forests. We define hyperparameter variables we would like to check online 3.

RandomizedSearchCV is specified as random rf in line 5, with an estimator equal to RandomForestClassifier, defined as the model in line 2. Param distributions are equal to param vals, defined in line 3; n iter represents the number of samples we would like to draw from all of the hyperparameter combinations, which are all set to 10. Scoring seems to be equal to accuracy, which means we are using accuracy as an assessment method for our model; cv is set to 5, which means we want the model to go through 5 cross-validations, and the ref In lines 11 & 12, we fit random rf to the training dataset & make predictions on the dataset using the right model using random rf.best estimator_.

Because 10 samples are taken from all hyperparameter configurations for each cross-validation, the total convergence rate equals n iter * cv, which is 50 in our example.

Random Search's Advantages and Disadvantages

Random search is less expensive in terms of computation. However, finding the best score from the sample space is not guaranteed.

Searching with Intent

Informed search is my preferred approach to hyperparameter tuning because it combines the grid and random search benefits. It does, however, have some drawbacks. Unlike grid & random search, guided search uses the following procedure to learn from past rounds.

1.   Perform a random search

2.   Look for regions with a high score.

3.   Conduct a linear grid search in a more limited area.

4.   Keep going until you find the best answer.

The genetic algorithm is a technique of informative hyperparameter tuning based on the concept of genetics in the actual world. We begin by making some models, selecting the best, then creating more models comparable to the best and adding randomness until we achieve our aim.

11.5 Genetic Algorithm is Implemented.

The library we're using is tpot, and the main inputs are a generation (the number of iterations to train for), population size, and offspring size. Look at the following example.

The TPOTClassifier is imported in line 1. The classifier is named tpot clf in line 2. The values for generations, population size, and offspring size are all set to 100. We can see the output of each generation (iteration) with verbose = 2, and cv is set to 6, which means we want to execute 6 cross-validations for every iteration.

We trained tpot clf on the training set & produced predictions on the test set in lines 6 and 7.

We haven't created any models because TPOTClassifier will choose the best model for the dataset.

Genetic Algorithm Benefits and Drawbacks

It takes advantage of both grid & random search, as previously mentioned. The tpot library handles calculating ideal hyperparameter values and picking the best model as the genetic algorithm adapts from previous iterations. It is, however, computationally costly and time-consuming.